No Time
- The Unofficia

John Fox

© Copyright 2020 John Fox

Contents

CHAPTER ONE - SHADOWS OF SPECTRE

The James Bond film franchise (based of course on the popular series of spy thrillers written by Ian Fleming) is a very special and unique series quite unlike any other. When it began in 1962 no one could have possibly dreamed that the Bond films would still be big business in 2020. There had been franchises before Bond - like Tarzan, Sherlock Holmes, Charlie Chan, The Falcon, Jungle Jim, Frankenstein, Lassie, Rin Tin Tin, Bulldog Drummond, Hopalong Cassidy, and many others. As the Bond series began, thrifty but fun franchises like Godzilla and the Carry On films were already becoming popular in their respective countries. The Bond franchise created by producers Cubby Broccoli and Harry Saltzman however was revolutionary. Previous film series operated strictly on the law of diminishing returns and lowered the budgets accordingly. They sought to extract every last penny out of their licenced property without actually spending any money. The Bond series reversed this tradition. Each new Bond film was bigger than the one that came before. More lavish, more expensive, more spectacular. It was a gamble that paid off handsomely.

Adjusted for inflation, the most successful James Bond film of all time is 1965's Thunderball. Thunderball marked the peak of sixties Bondmania but the series would still go on and on with enduring success and seemingly without end. On Her Majesty's Secret Service, the first Bond film not to feature Sean Connery, is often written about as if it was a dreadful failure but this was not the case. Sure, audiences at the time unavoidably missed Sean Connery but the film made some money and is now felt by many fans to be the best James Bond movie ever made. In the 1970s a new era of Bond was launched with the unflappable and urbane Roger Moore. Moore went on to make seven films (a record that is unlikely to ever be broken) and proved that the Bond franchise was a perfectly viable ongoing commodity even without Sean

Connery. The Bond franchise, with periodic recasting of the lead, could potentially go on forever. James Bond is much bigger than the actor who happens to be playing him. It is a brand as famous as any in cinema. James Bond is completely indestructible.

No Time To Die is probably destined to be remembered as one of the strangest films in the long history of this legendary franchise. Not so much for anything in the film or the production (although, as we shall see, the production was far from uneventful and the film's plot may raise a few eyebrows)but because of script and director issues and real world health concerns that have seen the release date for No Time To Die pushed back three times. No Time To Die completed shooting in October 2019 and is (at the time of writing) scheduled for release in April 2021. However, there is no certainty that even this latest date will be met. No Time To Die has been through two massive promotional campaigns, had a Super Bowl spot, released trailers, teasers, and promos, a dozen or more posters, featured in numerous magazines and websites, had a podcast, and released a theme song and music video. Bond fans could be forgiven for feeling as if they have been living with No Time To Die for years - only without actually getting to watch the actual film.

The original release date for Bond 25, before we lost the first director Danny Boyle, was November 2019. Bond 25 was supposed to be ancient history by now and a part of DVD shelves and computer streaming libraries. And yet, we are still patiently waiting for a cinema release that has been frustratingly on ice since April 2020. There is nothing that EON (the company who owns and produces the Bond films *) can do about the coronavirus epidemic. It is clearly not their fault that it isn't safe to release motion pictures in cinemas. However, taking so long to get Bond 25 into production clearly was their fault. It is difficult not to have sympathy with Bond fans who wish that the process of making these films could be accelerated somewhat so that the gaps between movies were much less frustrating. Long gaps between films is something that never used to happen in the Bond series (aside from a famously frustrating and long hiatus between 1989 and 1995 - which was due to litigation over TV rights and nothing to do with the producers or lead actor wanting a break).

Roger Moore made seven Bond films between 1973 and 1985. Timothy Dalton had two Bond adventures out in the space of two years. Pierce Brosnan's Bond films arrived in 1995, 1997, 1999, and 2002. It was only with the Daniel Craig era of Bond that production of these movies became what you might describe as sporadic. Quantum of Solace, in the Bond tradition, arrived in 2008 - two years after Casino Royale. It was after Quantum that the frustration began. Bond fans then had to wait four years for the next entry - Skyfall. Fans then had to wait three years for Spectre. Fans were then expected to wait FIVE years for Bond 25 - until the coronavirus threatened to make this wait even longer. The gaps between Bond films in the Craig era had become far too long. Cubby Broccoli would not have sat on his thumbs for two years waiting for a Bond actor to decide if he wanted to come back or not in the way that Barbara Broccoli did with Daniel Craig and Bond 25. Cubby would have simply recast the part and got the cameras rolling again. No actor was bigger than the Bond franchise. The reasons for the long gap between Spectre and the start of production on Bond 25 were though, as we shall see, many and varied.

2015's Spectre (incredibly, one of only two Bond films released in an ENTIRE decade) did not manage to replicate the critical and box-office success of 2012's Skyfall. Spectre had Sam Mendes back in the director's chair, saw the return of Blofeld to the franchise, and had a budget larger than the GDP of an impoverished nation. Hopes were very high for Spectre. It was expected to be extra special. Spectre turned out to be rather ordinary though. This wasn't the great film that some fans were expecting. Spectre had an inconsistent tone and awkwardly tried to introduce some gadgetry and humour back to the franchise while still continuing the vaguely connected 'personal' elements that had run through all of the Daniel

Craig films. Something about the film didn't really mesh. The humour and gadgets felt out of place with Daniel Craig and the persistence with the 'this time it's personal' trope in the Craig films was starting to overstay its welcome. Craig's status as the 'backstory' Bond was beginning to become tiresome.

The last act in Spectre saw Bond and the MI6 team involved in various shenanigans in London before a rather tame climax that had Blofeld failing to escape in a helicopter. You'd think that a famed criminal mastermind like Blofeld would be somewhat more competent when it came to planning an escape from a large city. Jarring moments like this gave Spectre the feel of a film that had never quite been thought through and nailed down. The last act was indicative of a movie that had run out of screenplay and story altogether and was merely blindly fumbling its way through to the end as best it could. Daniel Craig was said to be unhappy with the way Spectre turned out. This would have profound consequences for Bond 25. If Daniel Craig had loved Spectre and been completely satisfied with the end product then there is every chance that he might never have returned.

The Rotten Tomatoes score for Spectre noticeably sank like a brick once it had departed from the cosy and forgiving haven of British film critics (you can generally rely on British film critics to give the new Bond film a pass - even if it clearly isn't one of the better ones). The box-office for Spectre, while perfectly fine by most standards, fell short of Skyfall to the point where the film seemed to be left in cinemas for a preposterously long time to inflate the final figures. It would probably not surprise you if, like Hiroo Onoda, the Japanese soldier discovered on the Pacific island of Lubang in 1974 unaware that World War 2 had ended nearly 30 years ago, a bedraggled and confused cinema somewhere was still to this day running daily screenings of Spectre.

Daniel Craig, famously, made some ill-advised off the cuff comments at the end of the Spectre shoot when he said he would rather 'slash his own wrists' than make another Bond film. This was clearly a stupid (not to mention offensive) thing to say and a consequence of being tired and sore after an exhausting six month shoot. Craig, in mitigation for his comments, would later say that he shot Spectre in constant pain because of a leg injury he suffered during the production. He'd also spent close to a year away from home and his family completing his commitments to the film (a Bond actor is obviously required to do extensive stunt training before the film and extensive publicity to promote the film after it is completed). Craig had even doubled down on the wrist-slashing comments though by declaring that he would only make another Bond film for the money.

Of course, actors are not paid in jelly beans. They, like everyone, desire money. Even so, it was a fairly classless thing for Daniel Craig to say. It suggested that Craig's only connection to the Bond films was his salary and that he didn't care about them at all. This was clearly not the case because he worked ferociously hard on the Bond films and took a great interest in the production and creative decisions. Craig's interview after Spectre was a classic foot in mouth moment on every level. He really wasn't thinking at all. One can only imagine the reaction of studio executives when they read Craig's comments. He came across as ungrateful and charmless.

Though never officially confirmed by anyone, there was a general perception at the time of its release that Spectre would probably be the last Daniel Craig Bond films. His comments in that unfortunate interview were obviously a big factor in this perception (as was Craig's reported participation in a 20 episode Showtime TV show called Purity - which didn't actually get made in the end) but there was also a strong sense that Spectre, whatever its faults, did serve as a reasonable way to put the lid on the Craig era and give his version of Bond a fairly definitive (and happy) sort of ending. It was hard really to see how much more could be mined out of the loose continuity of the Craig films. Maybe it was time for the franchise to undertake a soft reboot and head in a different direction.

What had been different and bold in the Craig era for a couple of films was in danger of becoming stale and tiresome after four movies. This is why Bond had an advantage over many other franchises in that it was an accepted tradition that the lead actor would constantly change while the series went on and on. The recasting of the lead actor naturally gives the Bond franchise a temporary injection of freshness and novelty. GoldenEye and Casino Royale were both evidence of this. The Living Daylights (whatever anyone might try to retrospectively tell you about the Timothy Dalton era) was also very well received in 1987. A Bond film that marks the debut of a new lead actor is always hugely anticipated.

The media love nothing more than speculating on who the next James Bond will be and the man who emerged as the favourite in this uncertain 2015/2016 period of doubt over Craig's future participation in the franchise was Tom Hiddleston. Hiddleston, best known as Loki in the Marvel films, had turned in a vaguely Bondish performance in the BBC miniseries The Night Manager. This was enough for rumours to abound, with some degree of certainty, that trusted sources had suggested Hiddleston had done a successful screen test (directed by Sam Mendes no less) and would be unveiled as the new James Bond by the end of 2016. Those who are familiar with forums and entertainment websites will have learned by now that the phrase 'from a trusted source' is to be taken with a dose of salt considerably larger than a pinch.

The Hiddleston stories came thick and fast but they were never consistent and they were never verified. One magazine claimed Hiddleston had been seen cosily chatting with Barbara Broccoli in an exclusive London gentleman's club. Another magazine said Broccoli disliked Tom Hiddleston because she found him too smug. The tabloids said Hiddleston had blown his chances because of his bizarre 'PR romance' with Taylor Swift. Even the veteran thriller writer Frederick Forsyth decided, for reasons best known to himself, to add his two pence to the speculation. "I got a tip the other day which I'll share with you," he told the Sunday Mail. "I understand Barbara Broccoli is absolutely no way going to pick Tom Hiddleston. No. Way." It was Hiddleston himself who poured cold water on the speculation. Hiddleston said that no one had approached him about playing Bond in the first place and we shouldn't hold our breath waiting for an announcement.

If nothing else, the Tom Hiddleston buzz was a reminder that taking on the part of James Bond is like playing the lead in Hamlet, Doctor Who, or Batman. Others have played the part before you and others will play the part after you. Speculation about the next incumbent is therefore inevitable, unavoidable, and endless. It is a constant background hum even when someone else actually has the part. Tom Hiddleston was not going to be the new James Bond. No one was going to be the new James Bond, at least not yet, because Barbara Broccoli was still fiercely determined to retain the services of the old James Bond. She had not given up on Daniel Craig making Bond 25.

Barbara Broccoli told Daniel Craig that he still had unfinished business in the part and there was still plenty of story left to tell in his era of Bond. She refused to take no for an answer. Craig, despite his Sean Connery style weariness for the part that had made him famous and incredibly wealthy, was eventually persuaded to return for a fifth and almost certainly final time. Money was unavoidably the biggest factor in his decision (you could hardly blame Craig for accepting the gold plated carrot being dangled in front of him by Broccoli and her step-brother and co-producer Michael G Wilson) but his dissatisfaction with Spectre played a part too. Bond 25 would give him the chance to go out on a better film. Or so he hoped.

The loyalty and devotion of Barbara Broccoli to Daniel Craig could never be overestimated. Daniel Craig was unveiled as Bond in 2005 but the genesis of his casting went way back to 1998. It was in 1998 that Barbara Broccoli first became aware of Daniel Craig when she watched the film Elizabeth. Broccoli was captivated by this stocky fair-haired actor with the face of a boxer. She watched everything Craig had done and decided that he could be Bond one day - as soon as possible in fact. The only obstacle (and hardly a minor one in the grand scheme of things) was Pierce Brosnan - a popular and successful Bond who was only two films into his tenure in 1998. Brosnan was a fairly ageless type of actor who could conceivably have played Bond for another decade (which was remarkable really when you consider that Brosnan first slipped onto the radar of Barbara's father Cubby Broccoli in the early 1980s and had been cast in 1986 for The Living Daylights until a renewed television contract on Remington Steele forced him to make way for Timothy Dalton).

Barbara Broccoli's big chance to put Brosnan (who was the last ever James Bond actor to be cast while her father Cubby was still alive) in the ejector seat came after 2002's Die Another Day. Die Another Day, though profitable, was an especially silly entry in the series and seemed to indicate that a rethink of the franchise was in order. Die Another Day (believe it or not) earned decent reviews in 2002 but few Bond films saw their reputation plunge so dramatically in such a short space of time. The obvious solution was simply to make a better film next time and allow Brosnan to gracefully bow out of the franchise on better terms. However, Barbara Broccoli didn't have the patience or the desire for this plan. She wanted to take immediate and drastic action. Broccoli and Michael G Wilson decided that a reboot of the franchise was the only solution to the creative malaise that had resulted in Die Another Day. They wanted to draw a line under Die Another Day and start all over again. This meant that Brosnan would have to be let go.

Barbara Broccoli and Michael G Wilson both had their own reasons for feeling that a reboot of the Bond series was an attractive proposition. Broccoli, for her part, desperately wanted to cast Daniel Craig as Bond while Wilson had always quite liked the idea of doing a film where Bond was a young agent new to the service. He had floated this concept in the

1980s after Roger Moore's tenure came to an end but Cubby Broccoli vetoed the suggestion (Cubby didn't like the idea of Bond as a 'rookie' and preferred to depict him, as per usual, as an experienced agent and so hired Timothy Dalton). The fact that EON had finally acquired the rights to Fleming's first Bond novel Casino Royale (previously adapted as a 1954 CBS television film and also as a big-budget headache inducing comedy movie in 1967) gave them a tailor made story to launch a completely new era of Bond.

It was all rather rough on Pierce Brosnan - who probably deserved better treatment. Brosnan later complained that he had been fired via a short telephone call from Barbara Broccoli and Wilson. He said he felt like he had been 'kicked to the kerb'. While no one would say that the Brosnan films, in terms of their quality, constituted an especially vintage era for the franchise, the actor had resurrected Bond in 1995 after a long hiatus and was exceptionally popular in the role. It was not really Brosnan's fault that EON didn't hire better writers and directors during his tenure. Brosnan was also frustrated by the fact that he never seemed to be allowed to exert any creative control of his own on the franchise - which was remarkable given that he became a successful producer himself. The sour note that ended Brosnan's tenure as Bond was a great shame because it robbed the franchise of someone who could have been a great ambassador and elder statesman for the franchise in the way that Roger Moore was in his last decades.

Daniel Craig was genuinely perplexed and baffled when he was first contacted by EON and asked if he'd like to do a James Bond screen test. He was a million miles away from the traditional tall, dark, handsome Bond template. Craig thought that the Bond people must have gone mad. Barbara Broccoli assured him though that she was deadly serious and wanted him to do an audition. She told Craig that if he got the part he could do it in his own way. He wouldn't have to copy or mimic any of the Bond actors that had gone before. This was going to be year zero for the franchise. A complete fresh start. Craig's main competition for the part of James Bond in Casino

Royale, once the long list of potential actors had been whittled down by numerous interviews, readings, auditions, and screen tests, was a fairly unknown young English born Australian actor named Sam Worthington and a completely unknown 22 year-old actor from the Channel Islands named Henry Cavill.

Sam Worthington and Henry Cavill were later both very successful in their own right after their unsuccessful brush with potential Bond fame. Worthington starred in big films like Avatar and Terminator Salvation while Cavill became Superman. Martin Campbell, the director of Casino Royale, was rather taken with Henry Cavill in the auditions and would have happily cast him as the young 'rookie' Bond the Casino Royale screenplay was written for. "Martin Campbell and I both enjoyed Henry Cavill's audition," said the composer David Arnold, who provided music for the Casino Royale screen test footage. "He had all the swagger and physicality but maybe, as he was in his early twenties, felt just a little bit too young. We thought he had great presence and we weren't at all surprised when he turned into Superman."

The chances of Martin Campbell getting his way and casting Cavill though were precisely zero. Barbara Broccoli had her heart set on Daniel Craig and she wasn't going to be denied. At nearly 38, Craig was a little on the old side for the 'rookie' Bond angle Casino Royale was supposed to be going for but this was overlooked in the end. Craig became Bond and the rest is history. Just over ten years on from Daniel Craig's casting in Casino Royale, he found himself in a similar position to the one Brosnan had been in after Die Another Day. Both actors had made four films and were much closer to the end than the beginning. Brosnan was not given a choice on whether or not he wanted to make a fifth film but there was no danger of this happening to Daniel Craig.

The silly season when it came to Bond 25 gossip actually began almost as soon as Spectre had come out. In 2015 it was reported by the Daily express that the Bond franchise was about to reboot itself back into the Cold War. The writers of the television show Mad Men had been enlisted to write a sixties set Bond film that would star Michael Fassbender as Bond. The story was complete nonsense of course. Development on what eventually became No Time to Die began in 2016. It is nearly always reported in the media and on entertainment sites that an unused Fleming title will be the name of the next film. Bond fans are used to reading that the next film will be called The Property of a Lady or Risico and yet it never is. Bond 25 seemed to escape the usual The Property of a Lady or Risico rumours though. Neither of these titles were ever floated around in connection with Bond 25. The remaining Fleming titles (The Hildebrand Rarity and 007 in New York) were never alleged to be in contention either.

Bond 25 was often said to be called Eclipse in the media but this was a false claim. MGM secretly seeded a number of potential titles for the film online months before it even started shooting. Eclipse was among these - as was No Time To Die. Eclipse may have been considered as a title but it was never chosen or championed. Eclipse was actually not a bad potential title for a James Bond film but it did have one big drawback. The third film in the Twilight teen vampire series in 2010 was titled The Twilight Saga: Eclipse. The film was often referred to as simply 'Eclipse' by Twilight fans and in reviews. This connection made Eclipse a far less original and attractive idea for a Bond title and explained why it was never chosen (despite the media speculation).

Bond 25 was also alleged at various times to be called Shatterhand and incorporate elements from Fleming's You Only Live Twice. Dr Guntram Shatterhand was an alias used by Ernst Stavro Blofeld. Despite the remarkable longevity of the Bond series there are a surprising amount of Fleming titles and scenes yet to make it into the film franchise. Even when the films were still using Fleming titles they tended to mostly ignore the source material and make up their own plots (though they plundered Fleming's books extensively for character names). There is, for example, little of Fleming's Moonraker novel in the Roger Moore film of the same name.

By contrast, On Her Majesty's Secret Service, which was surprisingly faithful to the novel, is felt, as we have noted, by many Bond fans to be the best film in the series.

The media ran with Shatterhand endlessly in their early Bond 25 coverage and often reported the title as fact - even when the movie was in production. Shatterhand was most likely considered (alongside many other titles) but it was obviously not chosen in the end. Shatterhand was the name of a side-scrolling action game for the Nintendo Entertainment System in 1991 so one might speculate that this link (though obscure) may have counted against it. Another reason why Shatterhand felt like a poor choice of title is that it would have marked the third time in a row that a Bond film had a one word title which began with the letter S. A little more variety with the titles at this stage was desperately needed. 'Spectre' still felt like a tremendously lazy and underwhelming title for the last film. Shatterhand had more punch to it than Spectre as a title but, all the same, it didn't really quite feel right to have three films on the spin with a similar sort of title.

The rumour mill began to churn early on Bond 25. Dave Bautista seemed to suggest he would be back as the henchman Mr Hinx but with no director or script yet it was impossible to say if this was going to happen or not. In the end it didn't happen. Andy Serkis was alleged to be in the running to play Blofeld if Christoph Waltz didn't come back but this was pure speculation. Attempts to guess who would sing the theme song began preposterously early when it was claimed that Lady Gaga was the favourite. It seemed highly dubious that the Bond producers would be worrying about the theme song when they didn't have a script or a director. That would be a ludicrous case of getting your priorities mixed up to say the least.

The Daily Mirror claimed Bond 25 would be based on a 2001 Bond novel by Raymond Benson titled Never Dream of Dying. The blurb for the paperback reads - 'James Bond, 007, finally comes face-to-face with his most cunning nemesis - the enigmatic, blind criminal mastermind behind the sinister organization known only as the Union. It begins when a police raid goes horribly wrong, killing innocent men, women, and even children. Bond knows the Union is behind the carnage, and vows to take them down once and for all. His hunt takes him to Paris, into a deadly game of predator and prey, and a fateful meeting with the seductive Tylyn Mignonne, a movie star with a sordid past, who may lead bond to his final target - or his own violent end...' The tabloids reported that the film adaptation of Never Dream of Dying was going to be shot mostly in Croatia. This was all news to Raymond Benson and another fake story. EON never even used any of the (superior) Bond continuation novels by John Gardner so they were highly unlikely to start sifting through Raymond Benson's back catalogue.

The Daily Mirror then outdid themselves when it came to printing nonsense by claiming that Bond 25 was going to feature a giant space rocket designed by the tycoon Elon Musk. Bond 25, according to the Mirror, was going to feature space battles and futuristic technology. Daniel Craig was said to be 'bursting with enthusiasm and excitement' at these fantastical plans for the next Bond film. The Mirror also said that the film was going to be shot in South Africa. To the surprise of no one, just about everything in this Mirror article was completely fictional. More credible speculation came at this time from Variety. They reported that Daniel Craig wanted Monica Bellucci to come back for the next film. Other rumours suggested that Sir Kenneth Branagh was one of the names in consideration for the next villain. Branagh said in an interview that he'd love to be a Bond villain. Surprisingly, despite being as much a director as an actor these days, Branagh's name was never thrown around though in connection with the Bond 25 director's chair.

More speculative news arrived when it was alleged that Bond 25 would mimic the plot of On Her Majesty's Secret Service and have Bond get married. The speculation that Bond 25 might be some sort of stealth remake of OHMSS was probably unavoidable. At the end of Spectre we saw Bond and Madeleine Swann drive off into the sunset. It was easy to anticipate a story where Madeleine Swann is killed and Bond goes on a mission of revenge against Blofeld and Spectre. That film would have written itself. However, it would have been too obvious. EON wouldn't have got too many plaudits for doing the exact thing that many fans expected them to do. It was also alleged that Bond 25 would be heavily influenced by the Liam Neeson action film Taken - which became a surprise hit. Taken was entertaining but a fairly grim low-budget affair. You wouldn't have thought this film would be the best template for a James Bond adventure.

Jump Cut reported around this time that there were signs of some activity from EON - although their plans remained vague. 'Daniel Craig's involvement in the next film grows tenuous, as replacement names emerge from Hollywood's ether; notably Tom Hiddleston gave an impressive performance during his James Bond screen test, otherwise known as The Night Manager. You would certainly be forgiven for believing that Bond 25 is just a mishmash of gossip, desperate pleas, and tabloid misinterpretations. With no Bond, no title, no director, and no whiff of a plot to speak of, it must be said that the future direction of the franchise seems very uncertain. Almost too uncertain perhaps? A few weeks ago a German aviation museum in Wernigerode confirmed that a Bell UHD-1D helicopter was purchased by the James Bond production company (Eon) and is to be transported to the UK. This is then followed by the Mayor of Dubrovnik (Croatia) confirming that the city and Eon Productions are in advanced negotiations for filming of Bond 25 to begin later this year.'

The helicopter in question though turned out to be a red herring. It was acquired by EON for a film but not James Bond.

A favourite story in the British tabloids at this time was that the model and actress Carla Delevigne (who was clearly the flavour of the month in 2016) was going to be the next 'Bond Girl' and play the female lead in Bond 25. While this was all wonderful PR for Delevigne and her agent it had not the smallest iota of truth. This was pure gossip. Delevigne, on the strength of her previous film roles, wasn't much of an actress and at (a baby-faced) 25 she would have looked awfully young sharing the screen with Daniel Craig - should he return. It came as no great surprise that - when it finally began production - Carla Delevigne was nowhere to be seen amongst the Bond 25 cast. The tabloids reported that Emily Ratajowski and Margot Robbie were the other favourites to be the next Bond Girl. This was purely based on betting odds though rather than any actual news.

The tabloids alleged that EON had a meeting with Tom Hardy to discuss him playing 007 while it was still uncertain if Daniel Craig was coming back as Bond. Furthermore, they claimed that there was a big 'beef' between Hardy and Craig and that the meeting was designed to 'prompt' Craig's immediate return because he would surely not want to see his great hated rival Tom Hardy replace him. The idea that Daniel Craig and Tom Hardy were like a modern day feuding Bette Davis and Joan Crawford was of course completely unsubstantiated and suspiciously speculative. It would certainly not be the last time though, as we shall see later on, that Tom Hardy would be linked to the part of James Bond (even as the Daniel Craig era rumbled on with no clear end in sight).

Other bogus (and familiar by now to Bond fans) gossip arrived when it was claimed by various 'sources' that EON were planning to sell the Bond franchise after the next film. The tabloids declared that once the last Daniel Craig film was completed and released, Barbara Broccoli was planning to get out of the Bond business and let someone else take it over. This type of speculation was nothing new at all. In fact, it was very old. Since the early 1990s there have been media stories that the Broccoli family were preparing to sell their stake in the James Bond franchise. Bond fans of a certain vintage would remember reading in the early 1990s that the

Hollywood producer Joel Silver was going to take over the Bond franchise and cast as Mel Gibson as Bond. None of this happened. Bond was back four years later with Pierce Brosnan and still firmly controlled by the Broccoli family. It was, despite the media speculation, patently ludicrous to think that Barbara Broccoli was planning to wash her hands of James Bond and walk away.

Barbara Broccoli had inherited the franchise from her father Cubby and spent most of her life in and around the production of James Bond films. It was true that Barbara seemed to have more of an interest in 'side projects' outside of James Bond than her father but the films she had produced away from the 007 brand barely elicited a flicker of interest or recognition from audiences. It wasn't as if she had developed some alluring powerhouse career outside of Bond that required her full attention. Ultimately, the Bond franchise was a family affair and it was hard to see why Barbara Broccoli would ever want to threaten that unique distinction.

Behind the scenes, Bond 25 would become the first Bond film to be distributed by Universal Pictures. Neal Purvis and Robert Wade (the 'stock' and often much maligned writing team on the modern Bond films) suggested in a very early Bond 25 interview that Spectre had closed an era in the Craig films and that Bond 25, even with Craig in the lead role, would be completely different and not continue the story arc that had run through all of his films. Purvis and Wade seemed to suggest that their ideas for Bond 25 would mark a return to the anthology style of old (where there was no real connection to previous films) rather than the serialised style of the Craig era where the narratives of his individual films were linked together as if they were telling one long story. This was obviously something that didn't happen in the end. Bond 25 was pretty much business as usual when it finally began shooting. The new film continued the (sometimes awkward and occasionally excruciating) strategy of desperately trying to knit all of the Craig films together.

One could argue that the Craig era (described by Michael G Wilson as a 'miniseries within the Bond series') reached a natural end with Spectre. The personal angle to the Craig films and attempts at an over-arching continuity had become, well, a bit boring. A fun stand alone adventure where Bond is neither a rookie nor a world weary veteran but simply James Bond (there's a novel idea!) sounded like an overdue palate cleanser. This was not to be though. Bond 25 would continue a story that most people could barely remember anyway. It was rather like making a Bond film in 1995 with Timothy Dalton where Talisa Soto was back as Lupe and the villain was an underling of Franz Sanchez.

It was reported in the media that Daniel Craig had been offered around £70 million to do two more Bond films more or less back to back. The chances of Craig agreeing to this (if the story was true - which it probably wasn't) were pretty much zero. It was enough of a struggle to persuade him to come back for one film. When Spectre was in preparation there was a lot of speculation that the writer John Logan had already written Bond 25 in parallel and that this would be produced at the same time as Spectre. This story was clearly mistaken. The logistics of making one Bond film represented a mammoth (not to mention expensive) task so it was hard to see them making two at the same time. The toll this would have taken on Daniel Craig was obvious and not something he was likely to have subjected himself to. It is believed though that John Logan did have one of the first vague and tentative attempts at coming up with a treatment for Bond 25. There would be many ideas and script treatments thrown around the EON offices before production began.

Bond producer Michael G Wilson said after Spectre that Craig was no longer under any contract to play Bond but they were confident that they could get him to come back. They did persuade him to come back but it took an awfully long time for that to be confirmed. Craig only officially confirmed he was coming back on an American chat show in August 2017 - two years after Spectre was released. EON's involvement in the 'side projects' The Rhythm Section and Film Stars Don't die in Liverpool further nixed any any chances of a speedy transition into Bond 25. Daniel Craig's participation in the next Bond was further confirmed when he was seen filming a 007 Heineken commercial early in 2018.

Bond 25 was significant because this would film be promoted as the last of Craig's tenure. It was practically unheard of for a Bond film to let the audience know beforehand that the actor wasn't coming back. Even Barbara Broccoli accepted it would be Craig's last film. You knew for sure it must be Craig's last film if Barbara Broccoli had come around to this. The fact that this was Craig's last film mitigated some of the frustration some (though of course not all) fans felt at having to continue a story arc from five years ago that didn't exactly cry out for a continuation. Blofeld becoming Bond's step-brother was a reveal so stupid that many Bond fans would have happily swept it under the carpet and pretended it never happened. A clean slate though could only come with a new actor. If Bond 25 featured Daniel Craig but ignored everything that happened in the previous four films this would be an admission by the producers that they had bored their audience into submission by pursuing this navel gazing avenue in the first place. This was obviously something they couldn't bring themselves to do.

One problem with Bond 25 was that, as the coda to an era, it wasn't an especially pivotal film in the franchise. Bond 26, so long as it had a new actor, would clearly have a lot more riding on it than a Daniel Craig swansong. If Spectre had marked the end of the Craig era and Bond 25 had been a fresh start then no one would have complained too loudly. One could argue that under this scenario Bond 25 would have been more anticipated. No slight against Daniel Craig or the team behind No Time to Die, but the first film of a new Bond actor is always a special event in the Bond series because of the pure novelty of seeing a new Bond in action for the first time.

No one was seriously going to walk into Bond 25 wondering how Daniel Craig was going to approach the role or play the part. There wasn't too much novelty left after already watching him in four films. The fact that Bond 25 was the last film before a fresh slate unavoidably meant that the fans were anticipating what the franchise might do next as much as they were anticipating Bond 25. Where does the James Bond franchise go after Daniel Craig? It's a question that has no easy answer - hence the curiosity and intrigue it generates. The main task of Bond 25 then was simply to justify its own existence.

* EON'S website states - 'Danjaq is the US based company that, with MGM, co-owns the copyrights in the existing James Bond films and controls the right to produce future James Bond films. EON Productions, an affiliate of Danjaq, is the UK based production company which makes the James Bond films. Danjaq and EON control the rights to all worldwide traditional Bond merchandising, and with MGM control the rights in other areas of Bond licensing such as location based entertainment.'

CHAPTER TWO - DANNY BOYLE

Skyfall and Spectre both had an aftermath where it wasn't entirely clear if Daniel Craig was coming back or not. This was partly because of Craig himself - who always seemed to project a strange ambivalence about the part that had made him famous and wealthy. You never really got the impression that Craig was a huge Bond fan in private. You couldn't really picture Daniel Craig on Christmas Day watching The Spy Who Loved Me with a paper hat on his head and a tub of Quality Street. Sam Mendes said after Spectre that Craig was done with the part and that the end of Spectre was designed as a farewell scene for him. However, it was reported too though that Mendes had an idea for Bond 25 (with Craig) and did have some vague discussions about returning but these came to nothing in the end. Mendes (as was apparent from Spectre) had reached a creative dead end when it came to Bond. He wanted to go and do something else instead - which turned out to be the World War I drama 1917.

Mendes later seemed to complain that he hadn't had sufficient time to craft Spectre to his satisfaction. He admitted that making two Bond movies had taken its toll and that it had been a difficult experience. "There has always been an element that Bond has been on the wing and a prayer," said Mendes. "It is not a particularly healthy way to work. When I think of them my stomach churns. It's just so hard. You feel like the England football manager. You think, if I win, I'll survive. If I lose, I'll be pilloried. There is no victory. Just survival." Sam Mendes said that the most difficult thing about making a Bond film was that Bond fans all had their own version of James Bond in their head. Whatever you did there would still be someone out there shouting 'stop getting Bond wrong!' like Alan Partridge. This was very true. Bond fans all had their own ideas of what James Bond should be like and what the films should be like. They had their personal preferences and likes and dislikes. You could never please everyone. You simply had to hope you'd pleased MOST of them. The fact that Bond fans were opinionated, knowledgeable, and (occasionally) argumentative was a good sign though. It showed that they still cared.

Now that Sam Mendes was definitely out, the most important position to fill on Bond 25 was the director's chair. Jean-Marc Vallée, David Mackenzie, Denis Villeneuve, Yann Demange, and Edward Berger, were alleged to be on the original shortlist of potential Bond 25 director names. Another named they considered was Cary Fukunaga - who had been in contention to direct (what became) Spectre before Sam Mendes decided to return to make that film. The most offbeat name on the list was the German writer and director Edward Berger. Berger had mostly worked in German television but his work was highly acclaimed and he had directed some films. Berger's Showtime/Sky miniseries Patrick Melrose (with Benedict Cumberbatch) was fairly well received when it arrived in 2018. Berger though does not appear to have been the favoured choice for Bond 25. He was not at the top of the list.

Christopher Nolan had already ruled himself out of directing Bond 25. A Bond film by Christopher Nolan sometimes feels like something that is destined to happen one day but when that will be remains anyone's guess. Bond fans couldn't help noticing his OHMSS riffs in Inception and the great love for The Spy Who Loved Me that Nolan often expresses in interviews. Christopher Nolan said that a childhood experience of watching The Spy Who Loved Me inflamed his passion for the escapist magic of cinema. He loved how big, spectacular and fantastical the film was and he had always tried to recreate that childhood experience of watching The Spy Who Loved Me in his own films. Associate producer Gregg Wilson (the son of Michael) has said they (EON) would love to have Christopher Nolan direct a Bond film one day.

Nolan is not everyone's cup of tea (some people find his films a trifle cold and humourless - not to mention confusing) but he is technically brilliant, very good at casting (who else would have championed Heath Ledger for the part of the Joker?), and clearly an inventive and ambitious director. "I've spoken to the producers Barbara Broccoli and Michael G Wilson over the years," Nolan said in 2017. "I deeply love the character, and I'm always excited to see what they do with it. Maybe one day that would work out. You'd have to be needed, if you know what I mean. It has to need reinvention, it has to need you. And they're getting along very well [without me]." Nolan's comments suggested he was more interested in a reboot of the franchise than the tail end of an era.

The Danish film director Susanne Bier, director of television miniseries The Night Manager, was another named linked to Bond 25 by the media. This could well have been where some of the fuel for those Tom Hiddleston as Bond rumours sprang from. Bier would have become the first woman to direct a Bond film had she been chosen. In a 2016 interview, Bier said "I would probably cut off my ear to do James Bond." Guy Ritchie, according to the Daily Mirror, was another director that EON sounded out about directing Bond 25. Ritchie, after making his name in the (rather tiresome) British comedy gangster genre, had seen his directing career fall off a cliff when Swept Away and Revolver were massive critical duds. He had managed to rehabilitate himself somewhat though with Sherlock Holmes and The Man From U.N.C.L.E. It's hard to imagine that Ritchie was ever top the pile for Bond 25. There were clearly much better directors than him out there who would be happy to have a stab at directing a James Bond film.

A fairly popular suggestion on James Bond forums was that Martin Campbell, who twice relaunched the Bond series in the past with GoldenEye and Casino Royale, should come back to finish off the Craig era. Asked if he might be tempted to come back, Campbell (rather vaguely) answered - "I don't know. I might be, so never say never. I didn't after Goldeneye. I don't know if it was sort of arrogance or whatever I don't know. I just sort of said no to it. I was pretty much offered every one after that. But I just felt that I was repeating it. Another control room to blow up; another nutcase taking over the world. Also there is something refreshing about starting a new Bond, and particularly with Pierce [Brosnan]. It was sort of a Cold War sort of situation then, and we had Judi Dench for the first time. So there was a kind of excitement to doing it. Casino Royale was the same thing. Much the same reasons, actually."

Martin Campbell was in his late seventies by now and seemed to be directing a number of television movies. After Casino Royale, he directed the 2011 superhero film Green Lantern but it was famously a huge critical and commercial bomb and probably put paid to Campbell getting any big mainstream Hollywood films again. Campbell later directed The Foreigner - a 2017 thriller with Jackie Chan and Pierce Brosnan. The Foreigner got some decent reviews and suggested that Campbell wasn't quite ready to be completely written off yet. Martin Campbell knew as much as anyone when it came to making a James Bond film. He would have been a safe pair of hands for Bond 25 but maybe EON felt it was time to move on and look for directors who would bring something completely new to the franchise. Campbell represented the past rather than the future.

Paul McGuigan, who had worked with Barbara Broccoli on Film Stars Don't Die in Liverpool and is best known for directing some of the best episodes of the Sherlock TV show with Benedict Cumberbatch, was another name alleged to be on a list of Bond 25 director candidates. The factor that probably went against McGuigan was that he hadn't proved he had what it takes to make a big budget film. The biggest films McGuigan has directed, like Victor Frankenstein and Push, were critical and financial disasters. The chances of Paul McGuigan getting the director's chair on Bond 25 always seemed slim despite his name frequently cropping up in speculation.

David Mackenzie was actually reported to be the favourite to direct Bond 25 at one point but this speculation proved premature. He is known for films like Hell or High Water and Outlaw King. "I met with Barbara a couple of times," said Mackenzie in 2018. "I really like Barbara, and I know [Bond writers] Neal Purvis and Rob Wade well. I'm from a military family. There are various things that could have connected me to that thing, but then I got busy and that's the last I heard. I haven't had any further engagement."

One person who wasn't considered for Bond 25 was Matthew Vaughn. Vaughn always claimed that he was supposed to direct Casino Royale until Martin Campbell came along but EON have never commented on this. "I had a lot of meetings on Casino Royale," said Vaughn. "So much so that the head of MGM offered me it. I had a 24-hour period where I thought I was directing Casino Royale." Matthew Vaughn's films were flashy and entertaining. They were cheeky and full of energy. He was capable of toning down his style though. If Matthew Vaughn directed a Bond you'd imagine it would be more in the vein of X-Men: First Class than Kick Ass - or even Kingsman for that matter. It was all academic anyway. Matthew Vaughn just didn't seem to be EON's cup of tea. Maybe he'd somehow blotted his copybook with the Casino Royale affair.

One person EON would liked to have considered for Bond 25 was the Danish director Nicolas Winding Refn. EON had wanted Nicolas Winding Refn to direct Bond 24 when it appeared Sam Mendes might not come back but the Danish director had declined the offer and made it clear he wasn't interested. This obviously ruled Nicolas Winding Refn out of Bond 25. Another director who was considered for Bond 24 (Spectre) was Tom Hooper - who is best known for directing The King's Speech. Hooper said he would love to direct a Bond film one day. However, Tom Hopper does not appear to have been a serious candidate for Bond 25. Hooper later directed the megabomb Cats so his stock has plunged somewhat of late.

David Yates, who directed the last four Harry Potter films, was another name in the Bond 24 mix who didn't seem to be considered for Bond 25. Yates was busy on the Fantastic Beasts movies anyway and maybe not the most exciting candidate to direct a Bond film. Hiring someone like David Yates would have been a safe rather than bold selection. Other directors alleged to have met with EON to discuss the possibility of directing Bond 25 were Colin Trevorrow and Joe Wright. Neither of these were confirmed though.

The person that EON really wanted was the talented Denis Villeneuve - the director of films such as Sicario, Arrival, and Blade Runner 2049. Villeneuve would have been a tremendous coup for Bond. His films are stylish and compelling. However, although he claimed to be interested, he simply didn't have the time to make Bond 25 because he was too engaged on his adaptation of the sci-fi novel Dune. "I said to Barbara [Broccoli], I would love to work with you and with Daniel, but I'm engaged [Laughs]. I will love to do it, honestly. I'm a spoiled filmmaker right now. I think Daniel Craig is a fantastic actor and I would like to, but several months ago I came into do Dune and I engaged myself. I committed myself and I'm someone that doesn't step back."

In the end it was Danny Boyle who was eventually signed to

direct Bond 25. Boyle confirmed his participation in March 2018. That same month he was also confirmed to direct the film Yesterday - which would obviously have to be completed before he could direct Bond 25. Bond regulars Neal Purvis and Robert Wade had written the first tentative Bond 25 script until Danny Boyle and his screenwriting partner John Hodge made their pitch. The Purvis and Wade script was jettisoned in favour of the new script that Boyle and Hodge were developing. Boyle is not a writer but he works closely with Hodge and feels that Hodge's scripts also reflect his own personality and style.

Danny Boyle is someone who likes to put his personal stamp on a film and make sure that his own vision strongly comes through all the different elements and creative contributions. This was, in hindsight, a red flag when it came to the nuts and bolts of Danny Boyle doing a Bond film. Cynics would argue that a big mainstream brand like Bond is film production by committee and that a free spirit like Danny Boyle would find it very difficult to impose himself in such a constrictive environment. While it is open to question whether or not this is a fair reflection of how EON work, the Danny Boyle Bond 25 saga does tend to suggest that there is a limit to how much creative freedom a director and writer coming into the Bond franchise can be expected to enjoy.

Boyle had apparently been under consideration to direct both Skyfall and Spectre so his selection was far from a spur of the moment decision. EON had always liked the idea of Danny Boyle directing a Bond film and now they had finally got their man. Back in 2013 though, Boyle had been asked about directing a Bond film in the future and poured cold water on the idea by suggesting that the huge budget and scale of a Bond film would stifle creativity and not really suit his style. One thing was certain. Bond 25 would not come in over budget and late if Danny Boyle was in charge. He'd deliver the film at breakneck pace and probably have some money left when it was all over. There was even speculation that this was part of the reason why Boyle had been hired. To keep the costs down.

The story of Danny Boyle's involvement in Bond 25 is a strange tale but probably not a surprising one. Boyle is an atypical sort of director in that he is famous but tends to avoid big budget mainstream films like the plague. Boyle is still best known for Trainspotting and 28 Days Later - two lo-fi inventive British films. Boyle's films are known for their energy and indie DNA. It seems that the less money you give Danny Boyle the better the film will be. Boyle won an Oscar for Slumdog Millionaire (which, in classic Oscar winning tradition, has already been completely forgotten by most of the people who watched it) and was the artistic director at the London Olympics - where he worked with Daniel Craig for that skit where Bond meets the Queen. Boyle's previous involvement with big budget films was brief and rocky. His adaptation of Alex Garland's gripping backpacker novel The Beach was a complete disaster. The film version of The Beach is tedious to the point of being almost unwatchable.

Off the back of his early success with Shallow Grave and Trainspotting, Danny Boyle was signed to direct Alien 4 (Alien Resurrection) in the late 1990s but, upon realising that he knew absolutely nothing about special effects and this new fangled thing called CGI, decided to make a swift exit. "I didn't know what I was doing, and I wouldn't have known how to handle all the special effects that would have been a huge part of it. So I backed out of it," said Boyle. "I was terrified of the special effects." Boyle said that his experience with Alien Resurrection put him off franchises for life. Until Bond 25 at least. Danny Boyle was then a slightly unexpected, even offbeat choice for Bond. There was no doubt that Boyle was talented enough to direct a Bond film it was just a surprise that he had agreed to do so. Making a James Bond film just didn't feel like a very Danny Boyle thing to do.

This though was what made a Danny Boyle James Bond film a more exciting and intriguing prospect than another Sam Mendes Bond film. Even Sam Mendes wasn't excited by the prospect of another Sam Mendes Bond film. Boyle's Bond film would have more of an X-Factor. We wouldn't quite know what to expect. Danny Boyle had a certain unpredictability that other directors of his standing often lack. Boyle is capable of switching between different genres (he has done dramas, fables, a road movie romcom, even a zombie film) and approaching a subject from a strange angle. It was anticipated that his Bond film would have some striking images and maybe some lo-fi street level action (which would have been very Jason Bourne). Danny Boyle was also good with casting and spotting new talent. He gave early roles in films to (at the time) unknown actors like Robert Carlyle, Ewan McGregor, Naomie Harris and Cillian Murphy.

Barbara Broccoli and Michael G Wilson issued a gushing press release announcing that Boyle had signed to direct Bond 25. 'We are delighted to announce that the exceptionally talented Danny Boyle will be directing Daniel Craig in his fifth outing as James Bond in the 25th installment of the franchise. We will begin shooting Bond 25 at Pinewood Studios in December with our partners at MGM and thrilled that Universal Pictures will be our international distributor.' MGM's Chairman of the Board of Directors, Kevin Ulrich, also issued a statement. 'Under the leadership of Michael and Barbara, we couldn't be more thrilled than to bring the next 007 adventure to the big screen uniting the incomparable Daniel Craig with the extraordinary vision of Danny Boyle.'

Chairman of Universal Pictures Donna Langley was not to be outdone and also released a statement. 'Universal is extremely proud to collaborate with Michael, Barbara and MGM on the international marketing and distribution of Bond 25. The unparalleled combination of Danny's innovative filmmaking and Daniel's embodiment of 007 ensured we simply had to be partners in the next chapter of this iconic series.' All was well on HMS Bond 25 then. Everyone seemed to be thrilled and excited by the signing of Danny Boyle. The ship was steady and the course was charted. What could possibly go wrong?

Daniel Craig, who seemed to exert a creative control over the franchise that his predecessor Pierce Brosnan lacked (a frustrated Brosnan couldn't even persuade the producers to hire Monica Belluci rather than Teri Hatcher for Tomorrow Never Dies), was clearly on the Danny Boyle bandwagon too. Boyle would not have been hired if Daniel Craig didn't want him. Craig was said to have the final say on Bond Girls, the music artists for the theme song, and - of course - the director. Danny Boyle was someone that Craig respected and trusted. Boyle's CV indicated that he was a fairly safe pair of hands to steer Bond 25 but 'edgy' enough too to bring some fresh ideas and his own style to the table. The more that you thought about it the more the selection of Danny Boyle made sense.

Not everyone thought that Danny Boyle was the best choice to direct Bond 25 though. Some felt that his 'livewire' style and hyperactive visual gimmickry might be distracting. There is no way though of knowing how Boyle would have approached the film or what a Danny Boyle Bond film would have been like. This was what made him an interesting choice. Boyle's films also had a fondness for unexpected narratives within the story. You might think you were getting one type of film but then have the rug swept out from under you. Shallow Grave and Sunshine both took surprising turns late on (which were a strength in the former and a weakness in the latter). Boyle and Hodge could be expected to conjure a few twists and surprises for Bond too. These surprises, when revealed, were clearly not to the taste of their new employers at EON.

Danny Boyle's Bond film was slated for a late 2019 release. Production was set to start in December 2018. The film is believed to have got as far as set construction (a Russian gulag set and a gigantic rocket was apparently under construction for Boyle's Bond film when the plug was pulled) when the news dropped in August 2018 that Boyle and John Hodge had left the project and the producers were looking for a new director and a new script. This was the film industry version of a big football club trying to sign a new striker on transfer deadline day. It wasn't good at all. Bond 25 was almost certainly going to be delayed by several months now. Danny

Boyle's time on Bond 25 lasted about six months in total. Boyle's version of Bond 25 is now like Edgar Wright's Ant-Man or Tim Burton's Superman Lives. A film that only exists in an alternate reality.

Danny Boyle's departure from Bond 25 was due to what is commonly known in the film industry as creative differences. EON simply didn't like the look of the script that John Hodge was working on - despite the fact that they had hired Boyle and Hodge after the premise of this (apparently estranging) script had been pitched to them. The friction came when the producers decided to order a complete rewrite of the script that John Hodge and Boyle were developing. That meant new writers (Purvis & Wade were almost certainly going to get a phone call) and John Hodge getting the elbow. Danny Boyle, who is not used to being micro-managed by finicky film producers, was not happy at all to learn that EON now didn't want to use the script that John Hodge was writing. Boyle decided to bail out while he still could and go and do something else instead. It was Alien Resurrection all over again.

As a result of Danny Boyle's departure, the film was pushed back to February 2020. EON couldn't possibly know this at the time but the delay would be an absolute disaster and cost them a golden chance to have a lucrative cinema run and then release Bond 25 to VOD and streaming at a time when most of the planet's inhabitants were confined to their homes eating cornflakes in their underpants and absolutely desperate for something new to watch. Hindsight is a wonderful thing but the bean counters at MGM and the Bond producers must dearly wish now that Bond 25 had managed to slip in under the wire (so to speak) and make that original late 2019 release date.

It was widely reported in the media that Boyle left Bond 25 because the producers rejected his offbeat choice of Polish actor Tomasz Kot as the villain. It was also reported that Boyle had fallen out with Daniel Craig. Boyle later denied that any of this was the case and said his departure was purely because the producers wanted a new script. "I work in partnership with writers and I am not prepared to break it up. We were working very, very well, but they didn't want to go down that route with us. So we decided to part company. What John Hodge and I were doing, I thought, was really good. It wasn't finished, but it could have been really good. You have to believe in your process and part of that is the partnership I have with a writer." It seems plausible that what EON wanted to do was remove John Hodge but keep Danny Boyle. This obviously proved to be impossible because of the loyalty Boyle had to Hodge. Boyle was understandably unwilling to merely be a 'gun for hire' and direct a new screenplay hastily cobbled together by a committee or Purvis & Wade.

It was also reported in the media that one of the reasons Boyle left Bond 25 was because he wanted to kill Bond off at the end (presumably rather like Wolverine heroically dies at the end of Logan). This story has never been verified by anyone though. The Sun twisted this story on its head and said it WAS Barbara Broccoli and Daniel Craig who had wanted Bond to die at the end of Bond 25 but Boyle thought this was a stupid idea. Tomasz Kot, the actor alleged to have created a dispute between Boyle and the producers, later confirmed that he had done a few audition scenes with Boyle for the part of the villain. He said though that this was the extent of his involvement with Bond 25 and he hadn't the faintest idea if his casting had ever been approved or indeed created any debate or friction.

Just to further confuse everyone, the French-American actor Said Taghmaoui claimed in the media that he had been cast by Danny Boyle as a villain in Bond 25 but with Boyle's departure now had no idea what was going on. "I was cast by Danny Boyle, and just now he left the project, so of course there's some uncertainty. We don't know who the director will be, and the producers don't know if they're going to go Russian or Middle East with the baddie right now. I literally just received a message saying: 'If they go Middle East, it's you. If they go

Russian, it's someone else.' It's the story of my life. Always on that line between something that could change my life and something that disappears." Said Taghmaoui later said though that this was all 'fake news' and that he had been misquoted.

What would Danny Boyle's Bond film have been like? What was it going to be about? Leaked call sheets suggested that Boyle's proposed Bond film had a Russian villain and a Russian leading lady. Boyle was also looking for a Maori actor who had combat skills to play a pivotal role in the film - possibly a henchman (though never confirmed - it might have been a friend of Bond for all we know). The script that John Hodge was writing for Boyle apparently had Bond incarcerated by the villain for a lengthy time. This was clearly something else that EON didn't like much. That sounds bold but it wasn't unprecedented. Bond is a 'guest' of Blofeld for a big chunk of OHMSS. Bond is also a prisoner in Die Another Day and Octopussy.

Other reports suggested that Boyle planned to shoot part of his Bond film in Canada because he needed some frozen wilderness locations. Some ice bound locations ended up in the version of Bond 25 that went before the cameras months later (EON now owned John Hodge's Bond screenplay and were free to use parts of it should they choose - maybe they picked up a few ideas even if they didn't want to use the actual story). Boyle's Bond film was said to have plans to shoot at Centre Point - a 34 storey building in London. A sequence where a helicopter lands on the roof of Centre Point was apparently planned. Russian actor and former mixed-martial artist Oleg Taktarov (who has appeared in films like Predators) was alleged to have tested for an unspecified part in Boyle's Bond film. The Times reported that Danny Boyle had sent location scouts to Nambia before he left the production. Some scenes shot in Africa were apparently under consideration.

Danny Boyle was widely reported to have been casting for a female villain in his version of Bond 25. Angelina Jolie was cited as someone he had supposedly met with and liked for this part. However, it was later reported that a bone of contention between Boyle and EON was that he wanted to cast unknowns and they wanted to cast big names. This contradicted the Angelina Jolie story. Angelina Jolie is not exactly an 'unknown' is she? If you were casting for a female villain it's hard to think of too many bigger names than Angelina Jolie. Jolie's alleged participation was of the gossip variety and speculative. Helena Bonham Carter and Sarah Paulson were also alleged to be in the running for the part of the female villain. Iranian actress Golshifteh Farahani was also linked to Boyle's film in the media.

Boyle was also said to be looking for an actress to play a young MI6 agent that Bond is a mentor to in the John Hodge script. The idea of a female MI6 agent was something that would also feature in what later became No Time to Die. Sophie Rundle, Ella Purnell, Antonia Thomas, and Lily James were alleged to be on the Danny Boyle shortlist of names in contention for the part of the young MI6 agent. The Daily Express reported that Benedict Cumberbatch was going to be in Boyle's Bond 25. This was something they'd picked up browsing Reddit and had no basis in fact. Mark Strong had also been linked to a part in Boyle's Bond film and stoked rumours by posting a picture of himself in the gym with Bond 25 related hashtages.

Playlist later claimed that EON and Daniel Craig didn't like Boyle and Hodge's proposed Bond film because they thought it was too humorous and light. They felt it was too much like Kingsman. While this felt like a stretch (the Kingsman comparison that is), it seemed plausible to think that the screenwriter behind Trainspotting and Shallow Grave was probably better at coming up with jokes than Sam Mendes and Daniel Craig. Production designer Mark Tildesley later described what Boyle was planning for Bond as 'extraordinary'. "Unfortunately Danny's crazy, madcap ideas didn't quite tie up with what Barbara and Michael had planned," said Tildesley. "It was definitely a good thing to do. Maybe another time though. I'm revving Barbara up to have another go with Danny. [He had] some extraordinary ideas, they just needed a little pulling together. Danny had ideas, and the ideas didn't work out, and that was just the way it was."

It was alleged that Boyle's aborted Bond film was set to be more British based and less overblown than most Bond films. EON, according to whispers, felt that John Hodge's script was too light on action and stunts. Boyle apparently wanted to have a Cold War element (but in the present day) and include tension between the west and modern day Russia (which is still firmly in the corrupt iron grip of the sinister pint sized quasi-dictator Vladimir Putin) in the story. Boyle later reflected that his love of the James Bond books might actually have been a detriment to actually directing a Bond film. His head was full of Ian Fleming stories but the producers wanted more of a modern and fresh take on the franchise. One might argue that a Bond film which tried to have more Fleming residue than usual might actually be a good idea and as 'refreshing' as anything new the producers came up with themselves.

Danny Boyle, for his part, seemed relieved to have got out before it was too late. "I learned my lesson that I am not cut out for franchises, otherwise you're digging in the same hole. I am better not quite in the mainstream franchise movies, is the honest answer. I learned quite a lot about myself with Bond, I work in partnership with writers and I am not prepared to break it up." Of Danny Boyle's departure, Barbara Broccoli would later say - "It was hard on both sides because we had mutual respect and admiration, but better to know [the differences] before you embark on a project. We worked together well for a number of months, but there came a point when we were discussing the kind of film that we wanted to make, and we both came to the conclusion we were not aligned. Movies are very hard to make when you're all on the same page. When you're not, it's basically impossible; We recognised that, and in a respectful way we realised that it wasn't going to work out."

Dany Boyle later seemed somewhat at a loss to explain why

EON had not gone ahead with the Bond film he was developing. He felt that he and John Hodge had come up with interesting ideas that were worth persevering with. Daniel Craig would later say in an interview that Boyle had come up with a lot of ideas that were not quite right for a Bond film - or a Daniel Craig Bond film at least. It is possible that Danny Boyle making a Bond film was always something that was doomed to run into trouble. Boyle is used to a degree of creative freedom and improvisation that is not is not really possible on James Bond - a franchise where everything has to pass through Barbara Broccoli's office before it is allowed to go forward. Boyle brought his customary energy and enthusiasm to Bond 25 but ultimately it wasn't meant to be. Broccoli and Daniel Craig simply didn't like the direction that Boyle and John Hodge were heading in. They wanted to start all over again with a new script.

CHAPTER THREE - CARY FUKUNAGA

After Danny Boyle's exit, Bart Layton and S.J. Clarkson were initial names linked to the Bond 25 director's chair in the media. Layton had won acclaim with the films Imposter and American Animals. In a radio interview around the time of media speculation linking him to the Bond 25 director's chair, Layton said - "I am in discussions about it. There's nothing more concrete. It's very flattering to be put in the mix for something like that, and – of course – we've all grown up watching Bond with our dads and stuff like that. Well, a lot of us have. I probably have got bitten by the bug of action film-making and all of the magic that comes with it. I mean, obviously my Bond was Roger Moore and when you're a kid that's your Bond. You don't really think about whether he's the best Bond." Layton (a documentary filmmaker by trade) would later claim he turned the job down because he felt too inexperienced to handle such a big project at this stage of his career.

S. J. Clarkson, had she been chosen, would have been the first woman to direct a Bond film. Clarkson had only made one film (the little seen 2010 Nigel Slater biopic Toast) but she was a television veteran who had directed episodes of high profile TV shows like Heroes, Dexter, Bates Motel, Jessica Jones, and House. Around this time, Clarkson was set to direct the next Star Trek film but this obviously never transpired in the end.

The Canadian director Jean-Marc Vallée (responsible for Dallas Buyers Club, Wild, and the TV shows Big Little Lies and Sharp Objects) was said to be high on Barbara Broccoli's dream list of candidates to replace Danny Boyle but he asked not to be considered because he was too busy with other projects. For a time it was reported that French-Algerian director Yann Demange, director of the acclaimed independent film '71, was the new front runner to direct Bond 25. It was alleged in the media that Demange had even began working on a script and scouting possible locations. Demange later denied this was the case though. He said he had a meeting with the producers but never pitched anything or got offered the position. Demange said the reports linking him to Bond 25 were flattering but wildly overblown.

According to a writer at Variety, Christopher McQuarrie was another name EON were looking at. McQuarrie had just directed the brilliant Mission Impossible: Fallout. However, this link was more gossip than fact. McQuarrie wasn't available anyway. He later signed up to direct two more Mission Impossible films. Edgar Wright, of Shaun of the Dead and Hot Fuzz fame, was also alleged to be on a list of possible candidates. Wright was an interesting suggestion and not entirely similar to Danny Boyle. Wright's films were famous for their energy and zippy editing style. He was good at comedy and could handle action. Wright was a Bond fan too and had cast Timothy Dalton and Pierce Brosnan in Hot Fuzz and The World's End respectively.

There were a couple of caveats with Edgar Wright though that might have put EON off. Wright said that his favourite Bond film was Live and Let Die. His second favourite Bond film was The Spy Who Loved Me. Wright was a huge fan of the more flippant and fun Roger Moore era of Bond films and might not have been a great match for the more gloomy and introspective Daniel Craig era. Wright also had his own version of Danny Boyle's experience on Bond 25. Wright had developed Marvel's Ant-Man film and even personally cast Paul Rudd. However, he left the project when Marvel tried to rewrite his script - leaving Marvel to search for a new director at the last minute. Edgar Wright, like Danny Boyle, was used to a certain amount of creative freedom that big franchises like Marvel and Bond didn't always allow one to enjoy. As it turned out though, Wright did not appear to be in the final Bond 25 shake-up.

In the end, Cary Joji Fukunaga was announced as the new director a month after Boyle left the project. Fukunaga directed the films Sin nombre, Jane Eyre, and Beasts of No Nation. He is also a former cinematographer. Cary Fukunaga sent Danny Boyle a nice message once he got the job. Boyle wished him good luck. There were no hard feelings. Fukunaga was a relatively bold choice for director. He was primarily known for his work on the TV show True Detective. It is fairly common today for film studios to recruit talent from a television background. The distinction between film and television no longer exists. There is no difference in prestige or quality. Most people would rather watch Stranger Things or The Boys than giant CG robots punching each other in the head in the latest Hollywood popcorn blockbuster and for that you can hardly blame them.

Fukunaga was no yes man either. He was the original choice to direct the recent film adaptations of Stephen King's IT but left the director's chair because he felt the studio were not allowing him to make the film in his own way. Fukunaga made history as the first American to direct a Bond film - a fact that seems absurd. It's hard to believe a Spielberg or John McTiernan was never given a crack at Bond somewhere along the line.

Fukunaga was announced as the new director in September 2018. "I've wanted to do one of these [Bond films] for a long time, so that's not new," he said. "So right now it's just kind of dealing with the shock that it's real and the honor obviously and now the responsibility."

Cary Fukunaga was released as the director of Stephen King's IT only two weeks before it was due to start shooting. Fukunaga later said that the studio making the film was worried that they wouldn't be able to 'control' him. He felt this as a completely unfounded fear. Fukunaga considered himself to be a very collaborative filmmaker and didn't understand why anyone would think otherwise. He was an interesting director in that he was difficult to pigeonhole and put into any particular box. Fukunaga had developed horror projects, made a detective drama, and even spoke of making a sitcom. Now he was directing a James Bond film. That was an eclectic range of jobs. Fukunaga liked the idea of hopping around between genres and doing whatever he found interesting. He didn't want to become known for simply one type of thing.

The fact that Fukunaga was the first American to direct a Bond film was strange but more of an accident than a set rule. There was never any stipulation that American directors couldn't direct a Bond film and that Bond directors must be British or from commonwealth countries (as Martin Campbell, Roger Spotiswoode, and Lee Tamahori had been). In the early 1990s, the American director John Landis (of Blues Brothers, Trading Places, Animal House, and An American Werewolf in London fame) had been under consideration to direct Timothy Dalton's doomed third Bond adventure until litigation mothballed the franchise for several years. Landis had been one of the many writers who worked on the screenplay for The Spy Who Loved Me so he was not unknown to EON. John Byrum, another American director, was also on the shortlist to direct Dalton's third adventure.

It was widely reported in the early 2000s that MGM had wanted the American director Brett Ratner (best known for the Rush Hour films with Jackie Chan) to direct (what became) Die Another Day in 2002. Ratner was not chosen in the end but he was seriously considered (although, in light of his somewhat disgraced status in Hollywood today, it is probably a relief to everyone that he was never chosen). The acclaimed American director Katherine Bigelow said she was badgered by Sony Pictures chief Amy Pascal to direct a James Bond film but declined these offers. Bigelow, had she been interested, would have become both the first American and the first woman to direct a Bond film.

Steven Spielberg was desperate to direct a Bond film in the 1970s and telephoned Cubby Broccoli to offer his services. Roger Moore said that Spielberg made his Bond pitch after his classic television movie Duel came out. Moore was sold on Spielberg but Cubby though wasn't convinced that this very young director (who had mostly worked in television at the time directing episodes of shows like Columbo and Night Gallery) was the best person to put in charge of a huge production like Bond. After the astonishing success of Jaws (which more or less invented the summer blockbuster), Spielberg became unrealistic as an option for EON because he would be too expensive. Spielberg, once he became 'hot' after Jaws, also insisted on the final cut of his films and complete creative freedom - which Cubby Broccoli probably wasn't willing to accept. Spielberg was definitely a missed opportunity but Broccoli could hardly be blamed for not realising the young man who telephoned to ask if he could direct a Bond film would soon be as the most famous film director in the world. Spielberg was able to satisfy his desire to make a Bond style film when he teamed up with George Lucas for Raiders of the Lost Ark.

The myth that American directors were not permitted to direct a Bond film no longer existed now that Cary Fukunaga had been hired. EON had never closed the door on an American director - it just never happened before for some reason or other. Cubby Broccoli tended to rely on a fairly small circle of British directors that he knew and trusted. Terence Young,

Guy Hamilton, and Lewis Gilbert all made more than one Bond film though Peter Hunt, who was an editor on the Bond series, only directed On Her Majesty's Secret Service. All of the 1980s Bonds were directed by John Glen - who was previously the second unit director on the Bond franchise. One could argue that Cubby was quite conservative when it came to selecting directors. He tended to favour experienced directors that he personally knew well. Handing the director's chair to John Glen in 1981 was probably the boldest thing Cubby did but by then Glen was something of a Bond veteran anyway. John Glen had more or less been groomed for this promotion. Cubby's preference for choosing people he knew was hardly a negative though as all of the directors he used directed some terrific Bond pictures between them.

It seems evident from interviews with Martin Campbell that EON would have happily allowed him to become the modern day version of John Glen and direct as many films as he'd wanted to after GoldenEye and perhaps even Casino Royale. Campbell was probably shrewd though not to accept this offer. The experience of Sam Mendes on Spectre was plain to see. Campbell had a huge advantage over Mendes when he returned to the franchise because he was launching a new era (which, as we have noted, always gives a Bond film more novelty) and was also adapting an Ian Fleming novel. The film version of Casino Royale was not entirely faithful to the novel and had to include some new material but the basic nuts and bolts of the story were already in place. This was obviously not the case when Mendes returned for Spectre.

EON had managed to mitigate some of the damage to Bond 25 by finding a replacement for Danny Boyle in short order but they did have one big problem that couldn't be solved in quite such rapid fashion. There was now no script or story for Bond 25. They were having to start all over again from scratch. Fukunaga, as we have mentioned, had been in the running to direct Spectre before Sam Mendes returned and so already knew Barbara Broccoli and Michael G Wilson. At the time of his discussions to direct Spectre, Fukunaga said he would be happy to be considered again in the future even if they didn't need him this time around. The producers were grateful for this display of enthusiasm and, in their hour of need, turned to Fukunaga again when it came to filling the void left by Boyle and Hodge.

EON hastily cobbled together another gushing press release in which the name Danny Boyle was crossed out and replaced by the name Cary Fukunaga. The inevitable delay to Bond 25 was confirmed when Daniel Craig began shooting a film called Knives Out in 2018. Variety reported that Daniel Craig was to be paid $25 million for Bond 25 - if it ever actually started shooting. The new Bond film was now tentatively projected to be released in February 2020 rather than November 2019. Neal Purvis and Robert Wade were brought back to write a new script with Cary Fukunaga. As ever, it was the script that was proving to be the peskiest and most time consuming thing to get right on the new Bond film. This had happened before and it would inevitably happen again in the future.

When the Daniel Craig era began back in 2006 there was a sense that Bond had fallen behind the times because of the Jason Bourne films. The Bourne Identity, a 2002 Doug Liman thriller based on a book by Robert Ludlam, was about an amnesiac spy (played by Matt Damon) who travels through Europe trying to unravel his identity as a number of assassins and the CIA follow his trail. The Bourne Identity showed that you didn't need hundreds of millions of dollars to make a great action thriller. It had fantastic car chases, brutal fight sequences, and a compelling story. The Bourne Identity had a kinetic energy at times that the recent Bond films seemed to lack. 2004's sequel The Bourne Supremacy was also a critical and box-office success. The shaky camera style of new director Paul Greengrass was not universally loved by everyone but there was no question that The Bourne Supremacy was a rollicking ride and a terrific action film. The Bourne films were tough, mean, and lean and Bond, the producers decided, had to follow suit if the franchise was to stay relevant. The biggest single influence on the 2006 James Bond reboot was unquestionably the Jason Bourne films.

By the time of Bond 25 over ten years later, James Bond had
fallen behind the times again but this time the pace setter was
not Jason Bourne but, improbably, Tom Cruise. The Mission
Impossible films, amazingly, seemed to get better with each
fresh outing. They had gadgets, wit, fun, outrageous stunts. All
the things that the Daniel Craig era of Bond sometimes
seemed to lack. Bond had become old hat by not being Jason
Bourne and now it was old hat for not being Mission
Impossible. Fallout, the last Mission film at the time of
writing, had action and stunts to make the Bond team weep. It
wasn't just Fallout either. The previous Mission films Ghost
Protocol and Rogue Nation had raised the bar when it came to
stunts and the Bond movies were struggling to keep up.
Spectre's last act, where the MI6 team was fashioned around
Bond like the IMF team around Ethan Hunt in the Mission
films, was more Scooby Doo than Mission Impossible. These
scenes showed how the Daniel Craig era of Bond had gone
from trying to keep up with Jason Bourne to trying to keep up
with Ethan Hunt.

It wasn't just Mission Impossible that was catching Bond with
his trousers down. There was Marvel with Captain America:
The Winter Soldier. Winter Soldier is the closest Marvel have
come to making a spy film. It has twists, conspiracies, a
surprise villain, incredible action sequences, gadgets, and is
nearly everything that you wish a modern Bond film could be.
There was even Kingsman: The Secret Service - a cheeky and
very entertaining Matthew Vaughn fusion of John Steed,
Bond, and chav culture. Fast, fun, crude, unashamedly British
and deliberately wonky, Kingsman was a hell of a lot more fun
than sitting through Spectre. Matthew Vaughn had already
riffed on Bond in even more style with his prequel X-Men:
First Class. "I nearly directed a Bond [film]. And I didn't get
the chance, but you know, if you can't beat 'em, join 'em, or if
you can't join 'em, beat 'em, whatever the expression is," said
Vaughn. Bond 25 had to up its game when it came to action
and stunts. It had to compete with the other spy and action

franchises snapping at its heels.

Cary Fukunaga soon confirmed that Bond 25 would continue the arc that had begun in Casino Royale. This would not be a stand alone adventure with no references to the previous films (even though many Bond fans would surely have been fine with that). The planning stage of Bond 25 was set against some mild boardroom turmoil at MGM. While this was not insurmountable it was not a tremendous help either. MGM had most of their chips on Bond 25 and desperately needed the film to be a huge blockbuster. Fukunaga was said to be polishing the old Purvis and Wade script himself. Paul Haggis had previously 'polished' the script. Around this time the press also reported that Scott Z Burns had been hired to do an extensive four week script overhaul. Burns wrote The Bourne Ultimatum so he was no stranger to the spy genre. He was also known in Hollywood as an 'emergency script doctor' who had done some uncredited 'rescue' work on a number of troubled screenplays. It appeared that the script John Hodge was working on for Danny Boyle had been completely jettisoned in favour of new material. The Russian angle to Boyle's film had been quietly dropped.

Early news about Fukunaga's Bond film suggested that some location shooting would be done in Norway. Fukunaga seemed to reveal early that Spectre actress Lea Seydoux would be back as Dr Madeleine Swann. He was coy though about the Bond regulars Ralph Fiennes (M), Naomie Harris (Moneypenny) and Ben Whishaw (Q) for a time but most people expected them to return. The media reported that Fukunaga was looking for an actress to play an MI6 agent, an actress to play a CIA agent, and an actor to play the villain. Rami Malek was heavily linked to the villain role but his obligations to the TV show Mr Robot made his participation complicated and uncertain. Cary Fukunaga was reported to be chasing the Oscar winning actress Lupita Nyong'o for a role in Bond 25 but this did not transpire in the end. She simply wasn't available. It seems plausible that Nyong'o was pursued for the role eventually taken by Lashana Lynch. Lupita Nyong'o was all over the media when it came to casting rumours for Bond 25 but there was never any point where she came close to signing on for the film.

Early in 2019, Rami Malek won an Oscar for Bohemian Rhapsody - which only cemented the desire of EON to hire him if they hadn't already done so. Around this time it was reported that Malek was in final negotiations and a solution to his scheduling problems had been worked out. He would do both Mr Robot and Bond 25. This was nothing new. Michael J Fox did Back to the Future and Family Ties at the same time. Finn Wolfhard did Stranger Things and Stephen King's IT at the same time. Pierce Brosnan must be still scratching his head and trying to work out why he wasn't allowed to do Remington Steele and The Living Daylights at the same time. How about poor Tom Selleck? He wasn't allowed to play Indiana Jones in Raiders of the Lost Ark because of Magnum (not that I've got anything against Tom Selleck's Magnum - it's a fun show). Around this time though, a coy Rami Malek continued to deflect questions about Bond 25 in interviews. He did not deny the links though - which strongly suggested he had accepted the part.

A number of reports indicated that Bond 25, like previous Daniel Craig films, would shoot some scenes in Italy. The Italian website SassiLive said that a large part of the film would shoot in Italy and that Emma Stone and Dakota Johnson would be joining the cast. Neither of these actresses were even available and turned out to have no connection whatsoever to Bond 25. Rumours were high that Bond 25 would FINALLY start shooting in the first months of 2019. The new release date for the film was now announced for April 2020. Sources suggested that Bond 25 would start shooting in April 2019. Stunt training was alleged to be underway and locations had been scouted. The Swedish cinematographer Linus Sandgren announced late in 2018 that he would photograph Bond 25. Just before Christmas, Naomie Harris confirmed that she would return as Moneypenny in Bond 25.

While Bond 25 had not even started shooting, the tabloids had already started casting the next Bond themselves. It was reported that, on the back of the success of the BBC miniseries The Bodyguard, Richard Madden had met Barbara Broccoli and been offered the part of James Bond in Bond 26. This was news to Madden and Broccoli. "It's very flattering to be involved in that conversation at all," said Madden, "but it's all just talk, and I'm sure next week it'll be someone different." Danny Boyle even decided to join the next Bond sweepstakes himself when he suggested that Robert Pattinson (soon to become the latest big screen Batman) would be the perfect actor to inherit the 007 mantle from Daniel Craig. There would be plenty more 'armchair Bond casting' by the tabloids in the months to follow.

Daniel Craig's trainer Simon Waterson said that Craig spent a year getting into shape for Bond 25. His routine involved punishing workouts and a strict diet. A typical breakfast for Daniel Craig at this time was rye bread, poached eggs, avocado and kimchi, kale, and turmeric, lemon, and ginger shots. Craig would eat vegetarian meals for most of the week and abstain from alcohol. The newspapers reported that Craig was sometimes working out for twelve hours at a time to get in shape for the six month shoot. Daniel Craig explained the long gap between Spectre and Bond 25 as a consequence of him feeling physically 'low' after the last film and not wanting to put himself through such a punishing experience again. It was only the persistence and patience of Barbara Broccoli that had persuaded him to come back.

The Bond 25 team were now actively at work in Norway building sets and preparing locations. New comments from Daniel Craig around this time indicated that Bond 25 would definitely be his last film in the series. An earlier tabloid report that Barbara Broccoli hadn't given up getting him back for Bond 26 didn't seem very credible in hindsight. Craig would continue to be asked this question endlessly in the months to come. If Craig had a penny for every time someone asked him if this was going to be his last film he'd be even richer than he already is. This was definitely though the last go around. He wasn't going to be the Bond that cried wolf again. Craig's ambiguous nature when it came to doing the next film in the series stretched back a long way. This was nothing new though for the franchise. Back in 1979, Roger Moore suggested he would not come back after Moonraker but he ended up making THREE more Bond movies.

In March 2019, Barbara Broccoli was heard telling a fan that the film would definitely not be called Shatterhand - despite the media still acting as if it was! Ralph Fiennes appeared on television in March and said he still hadn't seen a script for Bond 25. He had no idea when he was supposed to start shooting his scenes. Fiennes didn't even know if a script existed yet. There were a number of stories around this time that Aston Martin would feature in the film again and that Cary Fukunaga wanted Bond to drive an electric car. No Time to Die (as it would become) would eventually feature (amongst many other cars) the Aston Martin Valhalla. In April, 2019, it was reported that product placement for Bond 25 would approach $100 million. Heineken, Bollinger, Aston Martin and Omega were the four main brands listed. Around his time, stories that Christoph Waltz would return as Blofeld began to appear. Nothing was confirmed though at this time.

The actor Billy Magnussen was also in the news with reports that he was being courted to play a CIA agent in Bond 25. Magnussen was indeed later cast in the film. His role was an anatagonistic one and his character would be on Bond's trail. Stories soon began to perculate in the media that the Bond 25 team would be heading to Jamaica. Meanwhile, a man alleged to be Rami Malek's stunt double dropped some less than cryptic Bond 25 hints on his social media. Malek had clearly been cast as the villain but they were desperately trying to keep this under wraps until the official press conference. Malek would later say that there was never any chance of him turning down a James Bond film. He thought it was a huge honour to be offered the part and looked forward to taking his place in the pantheon of Bond villains.

It was then reported that Phoebe Waller-Bridge was to provide a Bond 25 script polish in April 2019. Phoebe Waller-Bridge is an actress and writer best known for her award winning sitcom Fleabag. Waller-Bridge had apparently been brought in on the behest of Daniel Craig to give the script a bit more wit and improve the female characters. Craig got the idea to hire Waller-Bridge after watching Killing Eve. Killing Eve is a black comedy spy thriller television series based on the Villanelle novel series by Luke Jennings. The show has Sandra Oh as an MI5 agent who becomes obsessed with a psychopathic female assassin named Villanelle (a role which seems destined to catapult the charismatic and super arch English actress Jodie Comer * to future stardom). Waller-Bridge was the lead writer on the first (and most would contend best) season of Killing Eve.

There were some silly media reports (well, the conservative leaning Daily Mail of course) that this move was going to turn Bond 25 into some sort of postmodern feminist PC exercise in virtue signalling the audience to oblivion. A bemused Waller-Bridge was baffled by this and said that she was planning to change nothing major about James Bond. She was simply adding a few jokes here and there and making sure the female characters had a bit more life to them. Waller-Bridge said that her gender had nothing to do with being hired. Killing Eve was a darkly comic spy drama thriller so the participation of Waller-Bridge actually made a lot of sense when you stopped to think about it. If Bond 25 ended up with some of Killing Eve's dark thrills and black comedy as a consequence of hiring Waller-Bridge then that could only be a good thing.

"I had my eye on her ever since the first Fleabag, and then I saw Killing Eve and what she did with that and just wanted her voice," said Daniel Craig. "It is so unique — we are very privileged to have her on board. Look, we're having a conversation about Phoebe's gender here, which is ridiculous. She's a great writer. Why shouldn't we get Phoebe onto Bond? That's the answer to that." Phoebe Waller-Bridge was alleged to have been paid $2 million to polish the Bond 25 script - which is nice work if you can get it. It was later suggested that Phoebe Waller-Bridge was not quite a last minute addition to the writing team and had been working on Bond 25 longer than anyone suspected. Waller-Bridge had never read any of the Ian Fleming James Bond books prior to being hired. She started reading them as part of her research for 'tweaking' the Bond script. There were now apparently four people trying to hammer the Bond 25 script into shape. If one counts Paul Haggis and Scott Z Burns, then no less than six people had worked on the script.

* At the start of 2019, the Daily Mirror and other tabloids reported that Jodi Comer was the favourite to be the next Bond Girl in Bond 25. There was a lot of speculation that she would have a role in the film. The author Luke Jennings, who created the Villanelle character in the books, was publicly aghast at the thought of Jodi Comer becoming a Bond Girl though. "What a step down that would be. Craig is exactly twice her age. And is there a more nauseating phrase than Bond girl?"

CHAPTER FOUR - THE PRODUCTION BEGINS

The official press conference for the launch of Bond 25 took place on April the 25th, 2019. The location was not (as per usual) Pinewood but Jamaica. Goldeneye, Ian Fleming's estate on Oracabessa bay on the northern coastline of Jamaica, is the spiritual home of James Bond and made an appropriate place to announce that production on the new film was finally about to start. The press conference featured the producers, Daniel Craig, Cary Fukunaga, and some of the cast. Ralph Fiennes, Naomie Harris, Ben Whishaw, and Rory Kinnear were all confirmed to be back. Rami Malek was finally confirmed as the villain.

Malek was still in New York shooting Mr Robot so he had to send a video message. 'Hi everyone, this is Rami Malek and I'm not jealous one bit that you're all in the absolutely stunning setting of Ian Fleming's iconic Caribbean home Goldeneye, on the island of Jamaica. No, not at all. I'm stuck here in New York in production, but I am very much looking forward to joining the whole cast and crew so very soon. I promise you all I will be making sure Mr. Bond does not have an easy ride of it in this, his 25th outing. I can't wait to see you all soon. Cheers.' There was much speculation that Malik might be playing Dr No. His name in Bond 25 though was Safin.

Rami Malek had a lot of contact with Cary Fukunaga before he accepted the villain role in Bond 25. The reputation of Fukunaga was enough to make Malek sign up. He knew that Fukunaga was not making a Bond film for the sake of it and would only be directing Bond 25 if he thought he could deliver something good. Malek's conditions for accepting the part were that the villain should have no political or religious ideology. No one was planning to do this anyway so EON were happy to accept this condition. There was some criticism when it came to light that Malek's villain would have a scarred face in the film. Some felt this 'villain trope' was rather insensitive in this day and age. The idea that having a facial disfigurement or scar makes someone sinister or evil. It should be noted though that Bond himself has a facial scar in the Ian Fleming books. Rami Malek said that Safin's scars played an important role in the film. Safin was described as a villain who thinks he is a saviour.

The press conference was a strangely flat affair. A press conference announcing a new Bond actor would have been a very big deal. A press conference announcing a new Daniel Craig film about fifty years after the last Daniel Craig wasn't such a big deal. It is true that there have been gaps in the Bond films before but these were rare indeed. The only thing that compared to the long gap between Spectre and Bond 25 was the long hiatus after 1989's Licence To Kill. Litigation (over television rights) meant that it took six years for the next Bond film (1995's GoldenEye) to reach the screen. The dispute dragged on for so long that in 1994 Timothy Dalton got tired of waiting around and announced his departure from the franchise. It is sometimes speculated that Dalton was pushed (as opposed to jumping) because he was deemed by the studio to be an unpopular Bond. It is inconceivable though that Cubby Broccoli could have done this to Dalton. Cubby was a loyal friend and supporter of Timothy Dalton and they remained on good terms even after Dalton left the role.

The gap between Spectre and Bond 25 was almost as long as the gap between Licence To Kill and GoldenEye. This was absolutely remarkable because while the legal dispute had mothballed the series in 1989 there was no such excuse for why Bond 25 had taken so long to arrive. You can bet your life that if the litigation hadn't occurred then Cubby Broccoli would have delivered the next Bond film to cinemas in 1991. One of the reasons why Bond films do not arrive on a regular basis anymore is that Barbara Broccoli likes to take on other projects. She has, as we have noted, produced films outside the Bond franchise and has even produced plays for Daniel Craig. Her father Cubby Broccoli, especially when he became the sole Bond producer after Harry Saltzman sold his stake in the franchise, was happy to simply make Bond films and usually had one out every two years.

Barbara was more of a theatrical 'luvvie' than her father. You always got the impression that Barbara dreamed of the Bond films winning BAFTAS and Oscars whereas Cubby was simply happy to give fans a couple of hours of undemanding fun in the cinema every few years. Barbara could be grating at times when she was interviewed about a new Bond film. She could be pretentious. One would think she was producing Ingmar Bergman dramas rather than spy action films. There was no doubt though that Barbara Broccoli was a strong and determined custodian of the franchise. She was the boss. When Daniel Craig's replacement is announced you can guarantee that the new actor, whoever he happens to be, will have been personally selected by Barbara Broccoli. She will have the final say.

Cubby Broccoli and Harry Saltzman seemed to almost alternate their producing duties on the Bond films. If, for example, you read Roger Moore's Live and Let Die Diaries (which is an entertaining behind the scenes account of making his debut Bond film) you will notice that Moore mentions Harry Saltzman a lot more than he does Broccoli. Saltzman was obviously the more hands on producer when they made Live and Let Die. Michael G Wilson and Barbara Broccoli, who obviously had a family bond and shared history that Cubby and Harry lacked, were much more in harmony and worked together in a close partnership. The family legacy seems set to continue as Michael's son Gregg Wilson is plainly being groomed to take on a bigger producing role in the series moving forward. Barbara had served a long apprenticeship on the Bond films herself. In an interview for Bond 25 she later reminisced about working as a 'runner' on Octopussy back in 1982.

The constant on the writing team in the Cubby Broccoli era was Richard Maibaum. You never really got too much script chaos on the old Bond films (although the screenplay for The Spy Who Loved Me went through many hands) because Cubby Broccoli liked everything to be planned out in advance. Maibaum said that the key to writing a Bond film was to come up with the villain's 'caper' first and then the rest would fall into place. Interestingly, Richard Maibaum wrote a number of Bond films with Michael G Wilson. Wilson stopped writing on the franchise in the end though to concentrate on his producing duties. Michael G Wilson's experience of writing some the old films was made him a valuable person to have as a producer. Wilson had a good grasp of what would work and what wouldn't in a Bond film. This didn't mean there hadn't been some poorly conceived scenes and plots in the Craig era but then you could say that about any Bond film.

Wilson had a pretty remarkable journey on the Bond films. He played an extra in Goldfinger and then became a tax lawyer. After co-producer Harry Saltzman left the franchise in the early 1970s, Cubby brought Michael G Wilson (who was his step-son) back into the 007 business and Wilson had been there ever since. Wilson had also established a tradition of making a Stan Lee style cameo in every Bond film. Barbara Broccoli and Wilson now seemed more open to recruiting new writing and directing talent than her father had been. Cubby had his group of regulars and liked to work with the same people most of the time but Barbara was more willing to cast the net wider and take a gamble. Barbara was also (on the evidence of the one Bond actor she has cast) more radical and offbeat when it comes to casting Bond. You wouldn't want to put your neck on the line and try and predict who the next Bond actor might be because Barbara Broccoli is liable to completely surprise everyone again.

The biggest difference between the James Bond books written by Ian Fleming and the James Bond film franchise created by Cubby Broccoli and Harry Saltzman was humour. The films gave Bond (played by the peerless Sean Connery) deadpan quips and witty lines. Humour became an essential part of the franchise. Sean Connery and Roger Moore had impeccable timing when it came to dispensing the trademark Bond quips. These quips sounded less natural though coming from the mouth of Timothy Dalton. Timothy Dalton always seemed to be searching for a subtext in his lines but sometimes a quip is just a quip and didn't have to have any great significance beyond that.

Daniel Craig had a lot more in common with Dalton than he did Connery or Moore when it came to quips. The humour had been toned down in the Craig era to the point where any joke or attempt at humour almost felt jarring. Some fans felt that the Craig films lacked the fun of the old 'classic Bond' films and had become a bit of a drag. Films like Skyfall and Quantum of Solace didn't really have that Christmas Day afternoon joie de vivre of the old Bonds. Others though preferred the tone of the new films to the tongue-in-cheek

Bonds of old. It was purely a matter of personal taste. Cary Fukunaga, the man who loved watching Cheers as a child and dreamed of creating his own sitcom, was now the person who would dictate how much humour would be in Bond 25.

Fukunaga said in interviews that Bond 25 would be connected to the previous Craig films but still have its own identity and do its own thing. He didn't feel obliged to mimic any particular tone or style set by the previous four films. He was prepared to throw in an outlandish stunt sequence or joke into the 'drama' of the story that would conclude the Craig era. Bond 25 had lost some intrigue when Danny Boyle (who really knew what a Danny Boyle Bond film would have looked like?) departed but Cary Fukunaga brought some intrigue of his own to the table. It would be interesting to see what Cary Fukunaga might bring to the Craig films that hadn't been there before.

It would be hard to think of anyone who enjoys press conferences less than Daniel Craig. JD Salinger perhaps. Greta Garbo. Craig approached the Bond 25 press conference with all the zest of a man who had just been sentenced to life in prison at the Old Bailey. Cheer up Daniel, you felt like shouting at the screen. The cheque is unlikely to bounce! At least pretend to look happy. It wasn't just Daniel Craig. The cast and crew at the press conference seemed rather bored by the whole thing. In mitigation, one could argue that they were simply eager to get on with the film and found these press obligations somewhat tiresome at a time when they had so much work to do. The pagesix gossip site attempted to further deflate the (already deflated) press conference with some wholly unsubstantiated mischief. They quoted an insider as saying - "Everyone on the production side detests working with Daniel, he's so difficult and makes things impossible. But [Bond producer] Barbara Broccoli thinks he walks on water, and only her opinion matters."

No title for Bond 25 was revealed at the Jamaica press conference. Michael G Wilson said they often didn't have a title at the start of production on a Bond film and so this was hardly a new situation. That was debatable to say the least. Most Bond films have a title when they launch their first official press conference. A few months later it was reported that the press conference had planned to reveal the film's title as A Reason to Die. The night before the press conference the studio and producers had got cold feet about calling the film A Reason To Die though and scrapped the whole idea at the last minute. When it came to choosing a title, they had simply decided to kick the can down the road and think of one later. A Reason to Live, A Reason to Die was the name of a 1972 Spaghetti Western starring James Coburn and Telly Savalas. A Reason to Die being pulled as the Bond 25 title the night before made Michael G Wilson's answers at the press conference a trifle economical with the actualité - as Alan Clark might say.

New cast members Billy Magnussen, Ana de Armas, David Dencik, Lashana Lynch, and Dali Benssalah were confirmed at the press conference. Cuban actress Ana de Armas was to play Paloma - a CIA agent. Her role was not a huge one though. Ana de Armas is the first Cuban 'Bond Girl'. It was speculated that she was cast in the film by Daniel Craig because they had recently appeared in Knives Out together. However, it later came to light that Ana de Armas had met Barbara Broccoli several years ago and Broccoli had always liked the idea of the actress appearing in a Bond film one day. The 31 year-old Ana de Armas rose to prominence with her role as a holographic AI projection in the science fiction film Blade Runner 2049. Her biggest worry about doing a Bond film was her English but she felt this was getting better all the time.

The part of Paloma was largely crafted by Phoebe Waller-Bridge and a fairly late addition to the script. Daniel Craig said that Ana de Armas didn't have too much to work with when she arrived on the set but more than made an impression. Ana de Armas, given that she was not really playing a leading role in the film, later played a disproportionately large part in the promotional campaign. The marketing for No Time To Die (as it would become) often gave one the impression that Ana de

Armas was the main star of the film alongside Daniel Craig. The glamour provided by Ana de Armas was something that EON and MGM wanted to get full value for money out of.

The return of Christoph Waltz as Blofeld was not confirmed at the press conference. His return (surely one of the worst kept secrets in history) would only be confirmed in the trailer. English actress Lashana Lynch, best known for her role as fighter pilot Maria Rambeau in Captain Marvel, was to play Nomi in Bond 25. Nomi is a 00 agent who was recruited after Bond retired. Lynch was born in 1987. She made her film debut in the 2012 drama film Fast Girls. After toiling away in British TV and a couple more British films she appeared in the short lived Still Star-Crossed for ABC and then got a big break with Captain Marvel. The striking Lynch is someone who has been skirting below the fringes of stardom for a while and Bond 25 seemed set to be her big coming out party. The character of Nomi felt like a vague hangover from the Boyle film although Nomi was certainly not a young agent under the wing of Bond. Nomi was a full fledged 00 agent in her own right and Lynch had to go through nearly as many bumps and scrapes as Daniel Craig shooting the part.

When the media speculate who the next Bond might be they sometimes throw a few actresses into the mix as if James Bond is suddenly going to become Jane Bond. This would be as stupid as Lara Croft becoming Larry Croft. This recent speculation about a gender switch was probably inspired by Jodie Whittaker becoming the first female lead in Doctor Who. However, the Doctor is a regenerating alien. There is a plausible (as far as a sci-fi show can be plausible) explanation for why the Doctor (having previously been male) is now a woman. There is no such explanation for why James Bond should suddenly become a woman. Barbara Broccoli shot this speculation down in flames herself when she said that Bond would always be a man and she would prefer that new interesting roles for women were created rather than male characters become female. Bond 25 though would have, in Lashana Lynch, the closest we might ever get to having a female Bond.

It was announced that 26-year-old French-Algerian actor Dali
Benssalah would play Primo - a heavy that Bond first
encounters in Italy. This was the first international film
Benssalah had made before. Swedish-Danish actor David
Dencik was cast as Valdo Obruchev, a scientist who vanishes
and triggers the mystery in the film. Dencik said he had about
three months worth of meetings and auditions before he got
the part. Dencik had appeared in productions like Tinker,
Tailor, Soldier, Spy, McMafia, Top of the Lake, and Chernobyl.
He had been in a film with Daniel Craig before as he had a
small role in the Hollywood remake of the Swedish film (and
novel) The Girl with the Dragon Tattoo.

It is sometimes claimed that the Daniel Craig era of Bond
raised the bar when it came to attracting big names and top
acting talent to the franchise. This assertion seems somewhat
unfair though when you look back. The franchise, prior to
2006, had already featured actors like Christopher Walken,
Judi Dench, Benicio del Toro, Diana Rigg, Robert Carlyle,
Jeroen Krabbé, Christopher Lee, Halle Berry, Sophie Marceau,
Jonathan Pryce, Michael Lonsdale, Yaphet Kotto, Donald
Pleasence, Rosamund Pike, Telly Savalas, and Robert Shaw.
By any stretch of the imagination, that is an eclectic and
talented group of actors! It's not as if we'd never had good
actors or big stars in the Bond series before.

One area though where the Daniel Craig era did broaden the
horizon of the Bond franchise was the selection of directors.
Sam Mendes, for example, is someone you can't really imagine
directing a Bond film in the past. Although the gamble didn't
pay off in the end, Swiss director Marc Forster was a bold
choice for Quantum of Solace. It was equally brave to hire
Danny Boyle (who you couldn't really imagine being hired to
direct a Brosnan film in the 1990s) - even though we never
actually got to see what Boyle was planning to do with James
Bond. The Bond series today (and moving forward too one
would imagine) will always be looking to hire bigger name or

more radical directors than we got, for example, in the Pierce Brosnan era. With respect to Roger Spottiswoode and Michael Apted, you couldn't see them being hired today.

The crew for Bond 25 was listed as - Director of Photography Linus Sandgren, Editor Tom Cross and Elliot Graham, Production Designer Mark Tildesley, Costume Designer Suttirat Larlarb, Supervising Stunt Coordinator Olivier Schneider, 2nd Unit Stunt Coordinator Lee Morrison and Visual Effects Supervisor Charlie Noble. 2nd Unit Director Alexander Witt, Special Effects and Action Vehicles Supervisor Chris Corbould and Casting Director Debbie McWilliams. The film's huge budget (alleged to be $250 million) was offset by tax incentive schemes offered by the British and Norwegian governments.* No word on who might be composing the film was immediately divulged.

Of Bond 25, Barbara Broccoli said - "Bond is not on active service when we start the film. He is actually enjoying himself in Jamaica. He starts his journey here. We've built an extraordinary house for him. We've got quite a ride in store for Mr Bond." Broccoli was asked some questions about Danny Boyle but plays them with a straight bat. She said that they couldn't quite agree on the creative direction but declined to be drawn on any specifics. The official plot synopsis read as follows - 'In No Time To Die, Bond has left active service and is enjoying a tranquil life in Jamaica. His peace is short-lived when his old friend Felix Leiter from the CIA turns up asking for help. The mission to rescue a kidnapped scientist turns out to be far more treacherous than expected, leading Bond onto the trail of a mysterious villain armed with dangerous new technology.'

Because Bond films are always set in the present day, the producers and writers often tend to be somewhat pretentious about topical elements and reflecting the real world. While Bond films will sometimes use a news headline for inspiration, they do not really reflect the real world and nor should they do so. We go to see James Bond films to escape from the real world - not to be reminded that the world is a terrible place. One look at the news is all we need for that. Despite the occasional overblown claim by the producers that Bond must reflect the real world this has never really been the case. We never saw Bond fighting ISIS or battling child abusers or people smugglers. We never saw Bond fighting in the Falklands War. We never saw him fighting in the Gulf Wars. The topicality of Bond is a superficial sort of gloss that amounts to one of the writers calling Donald Trump a real life Bond villain or Barbara Broccoli saying that Bond women can no longer wander around in bikinis with a secret microtape stuffed down their underwear. Daniel Craig's Bond, for all the introspection, is no more a part of the real world than any of the other Bonds were.

The first reported day of shooting on Bond 25 took place in Jamaica. Daniel Craig was seen shooting some scenes with Jeffrey Wright - who was back as Felix. Craig and his stunt double Jean-Charles Rousseau were required to drive a battered Land Rover in some street market sequences. Lashana Lynch also shot some scenes during the Jamaica shoot. While the crew was in Jamaica they also shot some scenes that doubled for Cuba. These days it is impossible to make a film in secret and so there were copious photographs and reports in the media of Daniel Craig (in Barbour x Engineered Garments Graham Jacket and Vuarnet Legend 06 sunglasses) shooting his first scenes. MGM and EON were happy for these early reports because it was good publicity for the film and let fans and audiences know that - FINALLY - a new Bond film was now in production.

Craig was wearing an Omega Seamaster watch in the first leaked set reports. Bond was seen driving a blue Land Rover Series III in Port Antonio (where the producers and cast stayed during the shoot). This Land Rover had been seen in the Bond series before when it featured in the pre-title sequence on Gibraltar for The Living Daylights. Barbara Broccoli and Michael G Wilson gave an interview to the local newspaper while they were in Port Antonio. They said that shooting in the West Indies was a wonderful experience. It was great to finally get underway - although Bond 25 had already shot some scenes in Norway. It was a crafty ploy to shoot some stuff in Norway before the official press conference. This had made it slightly easier to avoid too much publicity and potential spoilers in Norway.

Daniel Craig said that Bond 25 went through four scripts before it started shooting. Baz Bamigboye, known for some fairly accurate Bond scoops in the Daily Mail, reported that even though shooting had begun, the script was still a work in progress and that everyone, including Daniel Craig, was working on the screenplay. The Daily Mail's source described Bond 25 as a 'well polished s***show'. Bond films (and films into general) going into production with the script still in flux is by no means new though. The 1997 film Tomorrow Never Dies had its entire script jettisoned as it entered production. Jonathan Pryce, who played the villain in that film, complained that he was suddenly given a new script that bore no resemblance to the one he had signed on for. 2008's Quantum of Solace, which was affected by a writer's strike, also began production with a script that wasn't completely finished.

Two weeks into May 2019, the Daily Mirror reported that there was tension between Daniel Craig and Cary Fukunaga. The vague evidence for this were some blurry photographs of the pair in conversation that seemed to feature some shoulder shrugging and finger pointing. At this time it was also reported that Daniel Craig had injured his ankle and flown to New York to have x-rays. He would be out of action for a while - leading to fresh speculation on whether this would delay the film again. Craig was shooting a dock scene when the injury occurred. This marked the second time in a row that Craig had injured himself early on in a Bond film. No wonder his wife was apparently fed-up with him making Bond films and going home battered and bruised. Injuries on films like this were nothing new though. Pierce Brosnan was injured sprinting on the set of Die Another Day and Tom Cruise broke his ankle shooting a rooftop stunt for Mission Impossible: Fallout. You can't wrap actors up in cotton wool on an expensive action film.

Making a Bond film represents a fairly unique physical and mental challenge for an actor. Production lasts about six months and as James Bond is obviously going to be in virtually every scene you can't expect to get many days off. Factor in the stunts, fight scenes, and generally getting battered and smashed around and you can see why Daniel Craig came to enjoy making a new Bond film about as much as a trip to the dentist. He had two teeth knocked out making Casino Royale, suffered a bad leg injury making Spectre, and now he'd busted his ankle on Bond 25. Craig was 51 when Bond 25 finished shooting. Only Roger Moore had been older while making an EON Bond film. Pierce Brosnan was 49 when he made his last film. Timothy Dalton was 44. Sean Connery was 40 when he shot his 'official' swansong Diamonds Are Forever. George Lazenby was 29 when he made his one and only Bond film. While Daniel Craig had never exactly relied on youthful boyish good looks (Craig was one of those people who looked mature even when he was young) and didn't ever seem to change much facially, his body was another matter altogether. This was the main reason why he had been reluctant to sign up to Bond 25 in the first place. He wasn't sure his body could take the strain.

Despite the concern, Craig was soon sighted back at Pinewood Studios and EON were quick to stress there would be no delay to the film. They simply had to shoot whatever stuff they could around the lead actor while Craig was injured so that the production did not get behind schedule. It was reported that Craig would require about two weeks of rehabilitation. The press reported that he had been operated on by the doctor who treated England football captain Harry Kane. Craig was seen with a cast on his foot at this time but images of him in the gym were soon released to signal his imminent return to action. For any medical buff eager to know more about the injury - Craig had an ankle ligament operation on his left ankle and suffered two ACL tears in his knees. The Sun's 'source' described Craig as a medical miracle man for fighting back from injuries that would have wrecked the career of world class athletes. Cary Fukunaga's main concern at this time was whether or not his leading man would actually be able to run in the film.

If anywhere can be called the physical home of James Bond it is Pinewood Studios. Pinewood is a film and television studio located in the village of Iver Heath in Buckinghamshire. 'The studio opened on 30 September 1936,' wrote The Guardian, 'with owners Sir Charles Boot and J Arthur Rank inspired by Hollywood to create a thriving British film industry, a desire that led to a series of mergers with other studios over the years - the first in 1938, when Pinewood took over Alexander Korda's Denham Studios. Pinewood quickly established itself as a location for great British films. The Red Shoes, starring Moira Sheaerer, was one of two Powell and Pressburger films to be shot there (Black Narcissus was the other). A year later, the first Carry On film, Carry On Sergeant, was filmed at the studio. It marked the start of 20 years of Carry On filming at Pinewood. Pinewood's greatest association, however, is with the James Bond franchise. The first film, Dr No, was shot there in 1962, and despite fires destroying sets in 1984 and 2006, Bond films have continued to be filmed at the studio. The Bond stage was rebuilt in 1985, the year before Pinewood's 50th birthday, and renamed the Albert R. Broccoli Bond stage in honour of the 007 producer.'

The news that Bond was back shooting at Pinewood was like an old dockyard hearing that the biggest ship in the fleet was moored there again. It wouldn't quite be the same without some shooting at Pinewood. There was trouble at Pinewood though in June when a Peeping Tom was discovered. A convicted sex offender (working as a maintenance man on Bond 25) planted a spy camera in the ladies' toilets of the studios. He was later tried at Aylesbury Crown Court and given 16 months in prison. It was reported in the media that Bond 25 would have an 'intimacy' coach for any love scenes. This was not officially confirmed by anyone though. Cary Fukunaga continued to do interviews at this time and said he was working 120% on the script to knock it into shape. The Bond production crews, like two allied army groups fighting on different fronts, were now simultaneously in Norway and back at Pinewood. The Norway scenes that had been shot so far were rumoured to be part of a pre-credit sequence featuring a young Dr Madeleine Swann. As of yet, Lea Seydoux had not shot anything for Bond 25. She was still busy on other films.

There was a lot of speculation that Madeleine Swann was going to be killed off early in Bond 25 - even though it was clear by now that this film wasn't planning to reheat OHMSS and serve it up to fans again in a different guise. The speculation that Madeleine was going to take a very early bath was unrealistic and wide of the mark. It seemed unlikely that they would go to all the trouble of hiring Seydoux (who is not exactly short of work) again and then bump her character off early. Her role in Bond 25 was going to be pivotal and important. The gamble of course was that Bond 25 was investing a lot in a character (Madeleine) and relationship (between Bond and Madeleine in Spectre) that most people had probably completely forgotten about already.

Bond fans on forums were talking about this stuff because they knew all the films by heart and love to discuss all the intricacies but casual audiences (who were expected to make up the majority of the box-office takings), unless they had recently rewatched Spectre, were liable to walk into Bond 25 without the faintest idea who Madeleine Swann was or why she was deemed to be so important to Bond. This, as Cary Fukunaga was well aware, was going to require some delicate exposition that had to be informative but not clunky.

The Daniel Craig era has what you can only describe as an awkward chronology in that Craig's Bond seemed to go from rookie agent to world weary veteran in the space of about one film. The Craig era seems curiously light on Bond just being an agent undertaking missions. It feels like a chunk of his 'career' is missing.

The only previous Bond films that deviated from the formula of Bond simply being a super agent before with a more 'personal' type of story were OHMSS and Licence To Kill. In the former Bond got married and in the latter he went rogue to avenge an attack on Felix Leiter. Bond films had brought back characters before (like Blofeld and Jaws) but they'd never attempted an ongoing continuity before in the way that the Daniel Craig films did. Licence To Kill makes no reference to The Living Daylights. There is no ongoing thread in the Brosnan films. The Roger Moore and Sean Connery films are episodic. The one film that cried out for a direct continuation, OHMSS, did not get one. OHMSS ends with the death of Bond's wife. However, the next film, Diamonds Are Forever, Sean Connery was back in place of George Lazenby and Bond's 'revenge' on Blofeld for the death of his wife is confined to the pre-title sequence. It is not even established though that Connery's Bond is the same Bond who went through the events of OHMSS.

Never before in the history of the franchise had the tenure of an actor attempted to tell one long story in the way that the Craig films did. Bond 25 was an attempt to thread all the Craig films together and give them some sort of definitive conclusion. If Cary Fukunaga considered this to be a hindrance to writing and directing Bond 25 it wasn't something he ever complained about. The opposite seemed to be the case. Fukunaga appeared to enjoy the fact that he had to pick up the threads of a story seeded in the previous films. The question of whether or not this experiment in continuity (if at times a rather vague continuity) through the Craig films was successful is a matter of personal opinion. It was fine for a Bond marathon but more casual viewers, as we have noted, could be forgiven for not having the faintest idea who Mr White was or barely remembering that Blofeld was in the last film.

Making the Daniel Craig films connected (as opposed to

traditional stand-alone adventures) was not really something that was planned or mapped out from the start. It was decided that, after the positive critical reception to Casino Royale, the next film (Quantum of Solace) would be a direct continuation and reference Casino. The producers felt a lot of goodwill after the reception to Casino Royale and so (understandably perhaps) chose to make the next Bond film connected to its predecessor in a way that the Bond franchise had never really attempted before. Michael G Wilson, in interviews for Quantum of Solace, constantly reminded audiences that this film was a direct continuation to Casino. His subtext was obvious. If you loved Casino Royale you'll love this one. Sadly though, things weren't quite that simple. Quantum of Solace was affected by a writer's strike and something of a mess (though I'm sure the film has its defenders).

The fact that Quantum of Solace referenced the previous film was something that would become a staple throughout the Craig era. All of the Craig films would be connected - in a fashion. One of the awkward things about Quantum of Solace was that it created a crime syndicate known as the Quantum Organistation to essentially act as a replacement for SPECTRE. SPECTRE and Blofeld were unavailable to EON for many years because of reasons we shall discuss later on in the book. The Quantum Organisation then became redundant two films later when SPECTRE and Blofeld returned to the series. The Quantum Organisation was a clumsy adjunct to the title Quantum of Solace - a genuine Fleming title that shouldn't have had to justify itself. That was all in the past now though. Bond 25 would be the last chapter in this experimental era and Bond 25 would, to get the most out of the experience, require some knowledge and perhaps even an emotional investment in what had gone before.

It's probably not completely accurate to say that the Bond films had never been connected before the Daniel Craig era. The Connery Bonds slowly develop Blofeld until he is revealed. Lazenby's Bond, upon his apparent resignation from MI6, is reminded of past (Connery) adventures through items in his office. The title sequence for On Her Majesty's Secret Service also connects to the past by showing us clips of characters from the Connery films. The intention is to assure us that while the Bond actor has changed this is still the same character. Even the Roger Moore films have some connective tissue when Jaws returns in Moonraker (as a consequence of the character proving to be so popular in The Spy Who Loved Me). The Craig era though was the first time the Bond series had attempted anything other than a very vague continuity. The Craig era relies on audiences to remember more about the previous films than you ever had to do in the past.

Rami Malek suggested in a June interview that he had already been to Norway to shoot a few bits and pieces for Bond. Malek said Cary Fukunaga was in Norway too when he was there. Leaked photos revealed Safin wearing a Phantom of the Opera style mask. Malek said this mask was important to the character. "We didn't pick a mask off a wall willy-nilly. We had to think extremely specifically as to what would make the most sense. If it doesn't make sense to the story and to the character, then arguably it loses impact." Cary Fukunaga said he drew on some Japanese aesthetics to create Safin's look and background. Some of the Norway sequences were being directed Alexander Witt for the 2nd unit.

A second unit director will typically shoot establishing location shots and some action sequences when the director is busy working with actors in the studio. Malek was shuttling back and forth while he completed his obligations to the television show Mr Robot. This was exhausting but he found the excitement and energy of being part of a Bond production invigorating and very rewarding.

Cary Fukunaga, in interviews for Bond 25, talked about how he had an idea that the end of 2015's Spectre all took place in Bond's head while he was being tortured by Blofeld in that chair. The end of Spectre could be a fever dream and Bond could wake to find himself still in the chair. This would be like the classic 1890 short story An Occurrence at Owl Creek

Bridge by Ambrose Bierce. It's hard to know if Fukunaga was joking but this was clearly an idea too far. One can't imagine that Sam Mendes would have been too thrilled to see the last act of Spectre written off as a bad dream! Fukunaga was not alone in apparently finding Bond's all too easy escape from Blofeld in Spectre to be oddly strange and dreamlike. It was one of the many elements in Spectre that didn't quite make sense.

Ben Whishaw did an interview in the middle of June in which he said he was due to start shooting his scenes for Bond 25 in two weeks but he still hadn't seen a script. Whishaw, with some dry understatement, described this as a 'bit alarming'. The newspapers also reported that, because of scheduling commitments, Rami Malik and Daniel Craig might not be able to actually shoot any scenes together. Well, look on the bright side, opined one wag, you never saw Captain Kirk and Khan together in Star Trek II and that turned out ok in the end. Malek said that the stories about him not being able to shoot 'key' scenes in person with Daniel Craig because of scheduling problems was completely fabricated and not true at. "The key scenes is something that was fabricated. But the thing is, Daniel was injured, so they are shooting what they can. I talked to Cary yesterday and the schedule has been altered. I know that. But with a franchise like this, I think they have it together. They have it figured out by now."

In June, a Bond 25 Behind-The-Scenes Featurette was released. This was a short promo that featured some behind the scenes glimpses of the film in production. The promo concentrated on the West Indian parts of the shoot. A happy and relaxed looking Daniel Craig was seen laughing a couple of times in the featurette - just to counter tabloid stories that he was a miserable so and so who didn't even want to be here. The aim of the promo was obviously to counter some of the mischief and negativity in the media. The message from EON was that Bond 25 was underway, it was all going fine, and everyone was happy and getting along with one another. While it was difficult to glean too much from such a short look at the film, there did seem to be an impressive amount of colour in the shots that we saw. It would be an impressive looking film if this promo was anything to go by.

Set visits to Bond 25 at Pinewood around this time revealed a lot of toxin vial props - which led to the obvious conclusion that biological or chemical warfare or terrorism featured in the plot. There was a mishap on the set in June when a controlled explosion damaged the 007 Stage at Pinewood Studios and left a crew member with minor injuries. The stunt was for a scene where a fireball rips through a laboratory. The resulting explosion damaged part of the roof of the 007 stage and blasted off five huge panels from the outside of the building. The British Health and Safety Executive, according to press reports, launched an investigation and gave the Bond 'bosses' a telling off. The Sun newspaper managed to get some photographs taken inside the sound stage as part of their story. The photographs merely seemed to show some scaffolding though. There wasn't much evidence of the laboratory set.

The Sun told its readers that there had been three loud deafening bangs and one crew member had almost been crushed by debris. It was 'utter chaos' The Sun reported via the usual unverified 'insider'. The Daily Mail went even further and said that Daniel Craig had said 'this isn't going to blow me up is it?' prior to the accident. Bond fans could rest easy though. Daniel Craig had not been blown up on the set of Bond 25 like Wile E. Coyote in a Road Runner cartoon. The newspaper reports were inconsistent and didn't really seem to know what had actually happened in the studio. In the end no official investigation was launched by the authorities - although a number of fire engines and ambulances had rushed to the studio after the explosion. EON nearly blowing up the 007 sound stage at Pinewood led to more idle newspaper speculation over whether or not the production might be cursed. These short memories are illustrated by the fact that MOST Bond productions (and film productions in general) are like this anyway.

Meanwhile, it was reported that Phoebe Waller-Bridge had finished her work on the Bond 25 screenplay and was no longer required for any rewrites. A lot of shooting was done in London in the back end of June 2019. Whitehall and Hammersmith were among the locations. Daniel Craig and Ralph Fiennes were seen outside the Rutland Arms in Hammersmith shooting a scene where Bond has a secret meeting with M. Rory Kinnear was also seen on the set. A still released by EON showed Daniel Craig getting out of an Aston Martin V8. These images confirmed that Bond would be wearing Tom Ford suits in the film. He also had a pair of Barton Perreira Joe sunglasses. The eagle-eyed would have spotted that Bond had a Benson & Clegg Plain Slim Rhodium Tie Slide.

Aston Martin confirmed that the DB5, DBS Superleggera, and Valhalla models would feature in the film. Daniel Craig had clearly recovered well enough from his busted ankle to get back into the swing of things. He didn't really have much choice in the matter. They could hardly finish Bond 25 without Craig. As before, Daniel Craig would have to ignore the pain and keep going until the film was in the can. After four Bond films he was starting to get used to it.

* A report in the Guardian suggested that the companies behind the Bond films had dodged paying their fair share of tax in Britain - despite the franchise being based at Pinewood. EON Productions disputed this was the case though and pointed out that the Bond films had provided a large amount of jobs and investment for the British film industry.

'From Miss Moneypenny to Q, James Bond has long relied upon a series of government officials,' wrote the Guardian. 'Now it has emerged that Her Majesty's most famous secret agent has also enjoyed the support of another British civil servant: the taxman. A new report by the investigative thinktank, TaxWatch, suggests EON Productions, the London-based studio that makes the James Bond films, makes very little profit in the UK but has received tens of millions of pounds in tax credits. Publicly available accounts reveal that Spectre, which came out in 2015, received £30m in tax credits, while the latest film, No Time To Die, whose release has been put back until next year because of the global pandemic, was handed £47m. The total amount of UK tax credits EON received since the credits were introduced in 2007 is likely to be closer to the £120m mark. Leaked emails revealed that 2012's Skyfall received £24m in tax credits, while TaxWatch calculates that Quantum of Solace (2008) would have received around £21m.

'"With cinemas and theatres around the country closing, and cultural sector workers facing real hardship, you have to wonder whether handing over tens of millions of pounds to such a profitable franchise is the best use of public money," said George Turner, director of TaxWatch. For a film to receive tax credits it must be certified as "culturally British" by the British Film Institute. But, then, few brands are as British as the 007 franchise which has generated some $16bn in revenues since it began. Daniel Craig memorably featured alongside the Queen in the opening ceremony of the London 2012 Olympics. While many parts of the films are shot abroad, production is centred at Pinewood Studios, near London. Editing and post-production work on Spectre was split between Pinewood and Soho in central London.

'Bond's political masters would prefer the spy was very much an exclusively British asset. In February 2016, Tory MP Mark Spencer said tax on the profits from the Bond movies "should be paid in this country, not all over the world". Danjaq said in a statement: "All the income from the James Bond films received by EON and Danjaq is subject to tax in either the UK or the USA. None of the income is sheltered in a tax haven." EON states in its 2015 accounts that once the production of a film has been completed, "the film is sold for a price equal to the total cost of production less the amount received in respect of UK Film Tax Credits". Such an arrangement is legal and common in the film industry. TaxWatch suggests it means that little profit will be made in the UK – reducing the tax liability that will accrue. How much tax Bond pays abroad is unclear due to the structure of the franchise's finances.

'But it is clear that it is hugely profitable. In 2014, leaked emails, believed to have been obtained by North Korean agents who hacked Sony Pictures Entertainment, revealed that Skyfall, which grossed $1.1bn worldwide, made $232m in profit for distributors MGM and Sony. Danjaq earned $109m. Spectre grossed $880m worldwide, excluding revenues generated from DVD and VOD sales. Danjaq said: "Since the 1960s Danjaq has chosen to make the James Bond films in the UK through EON Productions, resulting in the investment of more than a billion dollars in the UK film industry, the employment of tens of thousands of people, and showcasing the talents of British people to the world. EON has utilised the tax credits to help fund the making of Bond films in the manner intended by the government. This has enabled the Bond films to be continued to be made in the UK to the benefit of the UK film industry." "Every company in receipt of subsidy argues that the public money they receive is necessary to keep jobs in the UK," TaxWatch's Turner said. "The reality is that Bond has been produced in the UK for decades and many years before the film tax credit system was introduced."'

CHAPTER FIVE - THE END OF AN ERA?

In July it was announced that Dan Romer, known for his past association with Cary Fukunaga, would compose the score for Bond 25. This put to bed any lingering rumours that David Arnold might be asked back. Arnold hadn't worked on a Bond film since Quantum of Solace. Why the Bond team don't use David Arnold anymore is not really known but one could draw up some speculative theories. It could be that Arnold, after three Brosnan films and two Craig films, was becoming too familiar as a Bond composer and they just wanted to shake things up. Arnold, with respect, is a very good composer but he's not John Barry. The Bond franchise has never replaced John Barry and it never will (those majestic John Barry scores for the Bond films remain objects of awe and wonder) but replacing David Arnold was not such an impossible mission.

The other obvious reason why Arnold slipped out of favour with the Bond franchise is that new directors coming into the series understandably want to hire their own music composers. They want composers they know well themselves and who they know from personal experience will be a good mesh for their style. Sam Mendes wanted to use Thomas Newman for the music on his Bond films and Cary Fukunaga obviously had his own preferences too - which clearly didn't involve David Arnold.

The Sun newspaper continued its offbeat coverage of Bond 25 by reporting that the cast and crew were left fuming by Cary Fukunaga turning up to the set three hours late because he was playing video games. This was, even by the standards of tabloid newspapers, a ridiculous story. It conjured a mental image of Daniel Craig standing alone in his tuxedo looking at his watch while they all waited for Fukunaga to finish a level on Doom. Fukunaga was not willing to put up with mischievous tabloid tittle tattle of this kind and responded on Instagram by saying - 'There's not a minute on this job that isn't scheduled, and even during a shoot day, in the hours before call, between takes and setups, and after we wrap there's always a line of dedicated and hard working department heads hungry to prep our next sequences, no one sleeps on this kind of job. So sure it's hard, but it's still the best job in the world and I'd never disrespect the hardest working cast and crew. We're all in this together. As for my PS4 relationship, if my RDR2 progress is any indication, it's been stunted at 63% for months and if anyone spoils the end for me before I wrap on B25 I'm going to be p*****.'

The Daily Star jumped on the Bond 25 'pinch of salt' gossip gravy train in June by reporting that Daniel Craig had begged

Adele to come back and record the theme song. It was probably a bit early for the tabloids to start concerning themselves with who was going to sing the theme song. They hadn't even finished making the film yet. The tabloids were, as ever, endlessly fascinated by who might sing the theme song though. The new favourite was the young English singer Dua Lipa. Dua Lipa said she would love to sing the Bond 25 theme song but didn't want to 'jinx' her chances by talking about it. The other favourites at this time (according to bookmakers) were apparently Ed Sheeran and Jessie J. The tabloids said that Daniel Craig and his wife were 'rooting' for Ed Sheeran.

Prince Charles visited the Bond 25 set at Pinewood Studios on the 20th of June 2019 and met with the cast and crew. Prince Charles had last visited a Bond set in 1986. In 1986, Prince Charles and his former wife Diana, Princess of Wales visited the set of The Living Daylights and met Timothy Dalton and other members of the Daylights cast and crew. Prince Charles took a great interest in the cars on the Bond 25 set and was shown the Aston Martin by Daniel Craig. 10 DB5s were used in Bond 25. The car would have miniguns, a smokescreen, tyre spikes, and explosives. Prince Charles joked to reporters that he had been offered a cameo in the film and was now considering whether or not to accept the offer. You will not be surprised to learn though that Prince Charles decided in the end not to launch an acting career and accept a Michael G Wilson or Stan Lee style cameo in Bond 25.

Naomie Harris was seen for the first time in the media reports shooting scenes for the film at the start of July. She was pictured in the newspapers shooting some scenes with Daniel Craig in London. The scenes depicted Bond and Moneypenny arriving at a house to meet Q. This was confirmation that Ben Whishaw was now shooting some stuff too. Moneypenny was wearing a Paul Smith Black Check Pattern Mac coat and a Petar Petrov Blair silk-crepe blouse. Daniel Craig was later seen in July shooting some more London scenes with Ralph Fiennes and Rory Kinnear. Ralph Fiennes and Naomie Harris had met Prince Charles when he visited the production and media reports had some photographs of Prince Charles in what was clearly the set for M's office. This Pinewod based section of the production was clearly being used to get as many of the M, Q, and Moneypenny scenes scenes in the can as possible.

The Daily Mail reported in July that, in what they called a 'jawdropping moment', Lashana Lynch's character Nomi would be revealed to have inherited the 007 codename from Bond. Later reports though said that Nomi will be 004. The Daily Mail, rolling back on their original story, later reported that Nomi might not be 007 in the film because of a fan backlash. The fan backlash in question was mostly a figment of the Mail's imagination. There was no fan backlash against Lashana Lynch or her character. The fans hadn't even seen the film yet! This was the media trying to create a story where one didn't exist. It was something the Bond team were by now used to experiencing during the production of a new film. The concept of Nomi inheriting the 007 codename (if Bond was supposed to be retired) was perfectly logical. When a footballer player retires someone else has to take their number!

Meanwhile, media reports indicated that the producers had come up with an inventive way to prevent Daniel Craig from injuring himself. They had simply decided to CG his face on his stunt double to stop Craig from doing anything dangerous. Craig was generally depicted as the acting version of Frank Spencer or Mr Bean by the media during the shoot for Bond 25. July saw the production team head to Scotland. Filming took place in the town of Aviemore and Cairngorms National Park area. Some scenes were also shot at the Ardverikie House Estate and on the banks of Loch Laggan, just outside the park. A car chase was filmed at Ardverkie Estate, near Newtonmore and a helicopter was seen hovering overhead to capture the action. Pictures from the Scotland shoot saw a Toyota Land Cruiser being followed by Range Rovers. Scotland was being used to double for Norway in parts of the film. This was a pretty big car chase sequence with vehicles flying through the air and all manner of mayhem.

Bond 25 was not short of strange media stories and another one arrived when it was reported that Grace Jones had signed to appear in the film. However, it was then reported that Jones had stormed off the set when she saw how small her part was (what was she expecting? to be the lead!?). This story might sound like a classic 'slow day in the office tabloid clickbait' of the variety that plagues the production of any modern Bond film but Cary Fukunaga later seemed to CONFIRM the Grace Jones rumours. "I took a snorkelling trip with Grace Jones out in the waters in front of Ian Fleming's house when I was trying to woo her into being in the film," he later told Total Film. There was no news on whether or not Cary Fukunaga went waterskiing with Tanya Roberts or Alison Doody to lure them into the film.

The production moved to Italy in August to shoot in Maratea and Gravina in Puglia. As ever, the cast and crew on No Time to Die (well, Daniel Craig, Cary Fukunaga, and Lea Seydoux) were required to pose for press photographs in Italy to drum up publicity. Collider posted an article in which they said that Daniel Craig, Cary Fukunaga, and Lea Seydoux looked like bored sulking kids being forced to pose for holiday snaps by their parents. No one seemed to be having much fun. Yes, this was one part of the job Daniel Craig wouldn't miss. Press conferences and photocalls. In Maratea, Craig and Lea Seydoux were filmed by an onlooker shooting a scene where their characters have to cross some train tracks at a station. This appeared to be for a farewell scene as Madeleine got on the train but Bond didn't. It was also reported that the Bond production team had built a cemetery set in Maratea to shoot some scenes.

A big Aston Martin chase sequence was shot in Matera and some studio work was also undertaken while the unit was in southern Italy. 8,400 gallons of Coca-Cola were used to make a street in Maratea less slippery for a motorbike and car stunt (the coke left a sticky residue and so gave the bike and car more grip). Barbara Broccoli thought the stunt crew had gone mad when she saw that they'd covered the road in Coca-Cola so they had to explain to her why they'd done this and why they were spending a sizeable little chunk of the budget on preposterous amounts of this popular soft-drink. £55,000 was spent on Coca-Cola for this sequence. Coca-Cola, according to the stunt director, actually washed off very easily and made the streets look cleaner than they were before.

August also saw some shooting off the coast of the Isle of Wight in southern England for a naval scene. These sequences seemed tied into the fact that Safin has a submarine base that has to be infiltrated. Island Echo, the Isle of Wight's news website, reported all of the activity they'd seen. 'Fast boats, buzzing helicopters and a secret spy – it's like something out of a James Bond film. In fact, it is believed that producers of the next Bond film, have been filming scenes for the 2020 movie off the Isle of Wight this week. There has been an unusual amount of activity off of Cowes and Yarmouth over the past few days, with camera-rigged boats and helicopters zooming up and down each day. Island Echo understands that the filming has been for high-octane scenes in the forthcoming Bond film. A former Scoot ferries vessel, which is now used as a charter vessel, has been converted to carry a big budget camera jib. A flotilla of other vessels have also been seen in the Solent. It's understood that the boats are based out of Ocean Village, Southampton for the duration of their filming. Earlier this year it was rumoured that Navy-like boats were involved in filming other scenes for the film off the coast of Ventnor.' There was no sign though of Daniel Craig on the Isle of Wight.

Shooting was also done in the town of the town of Sapri at the start of September. The location in the film will be named Civita Lucana. Thankfully for the people of Sapri, EON didn't drench everything in Coca-Cola. The motorbike sequence was suggested by Daniel Craig at the last minute as he felt the film was lacking one more big 'trailer' moment stunt. A modified Triumph Bonneville Scrambler 1200 and early prototypes of the Triumph Tiger 900 will feature in the No Time To Die chase scenes. The motorbike stunt was performed by Paul "Fast Eddy" Edmondson - a former professional motorcycle enduro racer and a four-time World Enduro Champion. Edmondson had to hit an eight metre ramp at 60 mph to jump over a 22 metre wall.

The Aston Martin for Bond 25 was modified by special effects coordinator and Bond veteran Chris Corbould. A number of new gadgets for the car were floated (like drones) but many of these were rejected. Bond's Aston Martin DB5 now has GE M134 Minigun-style weapons mounted behind the headlights. "Q Branch gadgets on the DB5 include revolving M134 miniguns appearing from the drop-down headlights," said Corbould, "traditional smoke screen, mines dropping from under the rear bumper and an LED number plate creating a modern take on the Goldfinger revolving version." The Aston was pretty tooled up for Bond 25.

The Aston Martin has been an iconic part of the Bond series since Goldfinger. Sean Connery disliked the car because he found it small and uncomfortable but there was no doubt the Aston Martin looked terrific onscreen - especially equipped with Bond style gadgets. Roger Moore never actually drove an Aston Martin in his Bond films (although, curiously, he did drive one in the 1981 comedy film The Cannonball Run). It was decided when Moore became Bond not to immediately saddle him with too many of the iconic 007 trappings associated with Sean Connery. It took three films, for example, before we saw Roger in a naval commander uniform. The initial reluctance to invite comparisons between Moore and Connery was shrewd and helped Roger Moore to make the part his own. Roger Moore's Bond was associated with the Lotus but never the Aston Martin.

The Aston Martin returned for Timothy Dalton's debut film The Living Daylights and has been a regular part of the series ever since. We saw Brosnan drive an Aston Martin and Craig too. The Craig era though has seen you might describe as an over reliance on the Aston Martin - to the point where the car has arguably lost some of its novelty and become almost too familiar. Sam Mendes would wheel the Aston Martin out with a great fanfare in his Bond films as if he expected the audience to stand up and wildly applaud at the sight of a car they'd already seen dozens of times. You could actually make a case for the Aston Martin having a rest in the Bond franchise and the next Bond actor driving a different car for a change. Still, there few things as associated with Bond as the Aston Martin.

'James Bond's favourite carmaker was founded in a small London workshop in 1913 by the engineer Robert Bamford and the car enthusiast Lionel Martin,' wrote the Guardian. 'The name Aston Martin came a year later after their prototype successfully made it around the Aston Hill Climb track in Buckinghamshire. Aston Martin took its place on the international motor racing stage by competing in the 1922 French Grand Prix but the business ran into financial trouble over the next few years and was rescued in 1926 by a group of investors. It developed a competitive range of sports cars with an increasing reputation for engineering and design, entering the Le Mans 24 Hours for the first time in 1928. Production of its road cars was stepped up in the 1930s, with 140 cars built in 1937 – the highest prewar figure. The English industrialist David Brown bought the business in 1947, expanding operations and relocating production from Kensington to Feltham. Production was again moved in 1955 to Newport Pagnell.

'In 1963 the Aston Martin DB5 entered production and the famous relationship with James Bond was born a year later when it was made the car of choice for 007 in the film Goldfinger, starring Sean Connery. The character of James Bond has driven an Aston Martin intermittently on film since then, featuring in several films such as GoldenEye, Tomorrow Never Dies and Skyfall. The luxury carmaker changed hands a number of times during the 1970s and 80s and in 1987 the Ford Motor Company took a 75% stake. The DB moniker – David Brown's initials – was resurrected with the introduction of the DB7 in 1993, the year that Ford took full ownership of the company. Aston Martin opened a new headquarters in Gaydon, Warwickshire, in 2003, which was the first purpose-built factory in the company's history. It returned to the racetrack in 2005 with the DBR9, a race car based on the DB9 road car. In 2007, Aston Martin was sold again, this time to a consortium of two Kuwaiti investment houses, Investment Dar and Adeem Investment, for nearly £1bn.'

The task facing Cary Fukunaga on Bond 25 was to somehow make the Aston Martin feel exciting and fresh again. Fukunaga had high hopes that the Italy car chase would be a classic showcase for the Aston Martin and justify its return (again). If 2015's Spectre had proved anything it was that Sam Mendes was maybe not the most exciting director in the world when it came to car chases (Mendes had a really strange habit of shooting action sequences in empty streets). Fukunaga clearly backed himself to clear what was - when it came to car chases - a fairly low bar set by his immediate predecessor. There was a lot of excitement at the footage they'd shot for the car and bike scenes in Italy. Everyone believed that this would be a terrific sequence when it was all edited together and given a music score.

Former professional rally driver Mark Higgins drove the DB5 as Bond in the Italy chase sequence. He'd worked on previous films like Skyfall and Spectre. The car was specially built for the chase sequence with modern suspension and a new engine. As much as possible was done for real (as opposed to CGI). Some shots had to be done fifteen times to get them right. The chase was done on constrictive cobbled streets and required expert driving. All the cars used in the chase had BMW M3 engines. A total of seven DB5s were required to complete this sequence. One of the cars was driven via remote control so that Daniel Craig could merely simulate driving the car without having to worry about ACTUALLY having to steer and drive the car.

Coming up with new and original stunts is an almost impossible task after 24 Bond films - not to mention all the other action films that have stolen Bond's thunder and come up with Bond style stunts themselves. Bond has been in car chases, ski chases, motorbike chases, Bobsleigh chases, helicopter chases, speedboat chases. He's fallen out of an aeroplane without a parachute, had laser battles in space, been winched out of a helicopter, had fights in cargo planes, flipped a car on its side, driven a tank, had fistfights on trains, flown a jet fighter, bungee jumped off a dam, done a HALO jump, skied off a mountain, and (lest we forget) para surfed a glacier. Bond has had a car chase on ice, a fight on top of a cable car, driven a car underwater, fought in a battle on an oil rig, a battle in Fort Knox, a battle in a volcano. Bond has flown in a jetpack, jumped over alligators, motorbiked over a helicopter, flown a gyrocopter, driven a tanker truck. Over the course of 24 films James Bond has done literally everything it is possible to do in an action film.

How on earth do you come up with something that Bond hasn't done before? You probably can't really. All you can do is try to put a fresh spin on a stunt and make it as good as you can. One area where the Bond series couldn't really compete with Mission Impossible was the fact that Tom Cruise did most of his own stunts - however dangerous and incredible they happened to be. This gave the Mission Impossible films an authenticity Bond lacked because you could see that it was really was Tom Cruise (or Ethan Hunt in this case) there at the heart of the danger for real. Daniel Craig was doing his best though. He was seen, in a Massimo Alba Sloop Suit, bloodied and covered in dust (what else is new?) as he filmed scenes as Bond in Matera. Craig's stunt double was also seen getting blown through the air by an explosion. Craig had personally suggested using Massimo Alba for the fashion as he was a fan in real life.

The stunt and action crews on the Bond films were famously experienced and excellent at their job. It was no easy task for the Bond team to keep up with the competition but then this had been the case for many decades. Bond was essentially the first action franchise. It invented a whole new genre.* Without the James Bond franchise there would have been no Indiana Jones, no Jason Bourne, no Derek Flint, and no Ethan Hunt. Everyone from Steven Spielberg to James Cameron to Christopher Nolan was hugely influenced by the Bond films. The deadpan quips by Arnold Schwarzenegger in his classic action films were lifted directly from Sean Connery's Bond. The Bond series was also hugely influential in the many villains we've seen in action films through the decades. Alan Rickman's Hans Gruber in Die Hard is like the best Bond villain we never got. Shih Kien as the steel handed baddie Han in Enter the Dragon is patently a Bond inspired villain. Inevitably, though once a trend setter, the Bond series eventually became deluged with competition in the very genre it could claim (with some justification) to have invented. Sure there were cliffhanger serials and adventure romps before 007 but James Bond was the first movie series to do it on a huge budget and introduce the modern action tropes we still in evidence in the cinema of today.

It was unavoidable in the end then that the Bond franchise would itself start to be inspired by other films. Live and Let Die was influenced by the Blaxploitation genre (one could argue too that Live and Let Die is the only Bond movie that is influenced by the horror genre). The Man with the Golden Gun has some kung-fu scenes in deference to the Bruce Lee phenomenon. Moonraker was patently inspired by Star Wars. Licence To Kill has some scenes that could have been lifted straight out of Miami Vice. The influence of Raiders of the Lost Ark is evident in some of the stunts in the 1980s Bond films. The Daniel Craig reboot, as we have noted, was heavily influenced by the Jason Bourne films. Quantum of Solace took the Bourne influence to extremes and even tried to adopt the obstreperous camera and editing style of Paul Greengrass.

The Bond franchise has had to compete with an eclectic and constant number of action films and franchises over the decades. Many of these films and franchises were inspired by Bond themselves. The list of films and franchises the Bond series, over many decades, has had to keep pace with is endless and varied. Dirty Harry, Enter the Dragon, Rambo, Lethal Weapon, Superman, Die Hard, Mad Max, Arnold Schwarzenegger movies, John Woo, Speed, Mission Impossible, Batman, The Matrix, Derek Flint, Matt Helm, Bulldog Drummond, Remo Williams, The Long Kiss Goodnight, Lara Croft, xXx, Jack Ryan, Jackie Chan, Stormbreaker, The Peacemaker, Fast and the Furious, Marvel, John Wick, Taken. No other franchise or action character though has been as enduring as James Bond.

Aside from Mission Impossible, the other big action franchises in the Daniel Craig era have been the Fast and the Furious and Marvel movies. The connected nature of the Marvel movies has some parallels with the Daniel Craig era. It would be inaccurate though to say that they had an influence on the Bond series when it came to long form storyteling because the Marvel films only really kicked into gear with 2008's Iron Man - by which time the Daniel Craig era was already two films old and committed to a continuity (of sorts) rather than the usual stand alone adventures. Serialised storytelling is something that seems to be in vogue. The TV shows we binge require us to pay attention and remember what has gone before. Blockbuster film franchises like Twilight and Harry Potter used serialised storytelling.

The advantage the Marvel films had over the Craig Bond films is that they arrived on a more regular basis. The disadvantage with Marvel movies is that there were so many of them. If you missed a Marvel film (and most of us probably missed a few of them at the time) then the chances are that you missed an Easter egg that would be paid off in a future film. The Craig Bond films were far fewer and didn't really work like this. Even if you'd never watched Casino Royale or Quantum of Solace you could watch probably watch Skyfall and not feel too confused by anything. It certainly helped though if you had seen the previous films. The Craig Bond films were desperate to get us invested in a story that took more than one film to resolve.

At first glance it seems difficult to draw too many comparisons between Fast & Furious and James Bond but the car racing racing franchise, as it has developed, has riffed more and more on classic Bond films. Screenrant argued that the Fast & Furious franchise shrewdly mines the rompish fun of the old Bond films in an era when the modern Bond franchise seems to take itself a little too seriously. 'With Furious 7, the Fast & Furious series officially took over Bond's legacy. While 007 these days offers a more "grown-up" take on the spy genre, Fast & Furious saw the void left by Bond embarking in a new direction and took its place, offering viewers global adventure, imaginative setpieces, and unparalleled stuntwork. Furious 7 is a classic 007 movie with the lead character split across Vin Diesel, Paul Walker, and their combined "family." The action is incredible, and anchored in real life stunts, with minimal use of CGI throughout (yes, they really dropped a bus off the side of a cliff).

'Furthermore, the action is set in varied locales ranging from the streets of Los Angeles to the sandy paradise of Abu Dhabi. Even the extraneous shots of dancing girls during parties and street races have their roots in 007 films; no matter what, pretty much every Bond flick has at least one scene featuring a throng of bikini-clad girls sitting around being sexy, to say nothing of those legendary opening credits sequences. If we didn't know better, Fate of the Furious could easily be mistaken for a 007 movie. The trailer opens with what feels like a classic James Bond pre-credits sequence, and quickly moves on to the main story. Dominic Toretto is a rogue agent in the vein of Goldeneye's Alec Trevelyan, and Mr. Nobody serves as a replacement for M, 007's boss and mission control. Ludacris' character is Q, the master of gadgets and computers, and the rest of the team is essentially stand in for Bond himself. The trailer even culminates in an explosive car chase on a frozen lake, which is straight out of 2002's Die Another Day - though it ups the ante by substituting the ill-advised CGI windsurfing with a gigantic submarine rising out of the water and giving chase to our heroes.'

Another obvious challenge for anyone making a Bond film today is this: how do you give Bond an impressive new gadget in an age when everyone has an iPhone in their pocket? Michael G Wilson has admitted that it is exceptionally difficult now to give Bond a fancy new gizmo that will impress anyone in this age of high technology. Perhaps the relative lack of gadgets in the Craig era is not merely an attempt to make the films more grounded but a pragmatic reaction to the advancement of real technology? As such, Bond 25 would be light on 'personal' gadgets. In this day and age it would be very difficult for Bond to impress anyone with any pocket sized Q lab technology he happened to be equipped with.

In August, the Editor-in-chief of 'James Bond Brazil' (Marcos Kontze) took to Twitter and revealed a number of 'insider rumours' he had heard about the film. The British newspapers naturally cut and paste his claims and reported them as fact. Kontze's claims were questionable to say the least. He said that Sting was under consideration for the theme song. Sting? What was this, 1985? It was highly unlikely that Sting was in contention for a 2020 Bond theme. Kontze also claimed that Genoma of a Woman was under consideration for the title and the preferred choice of Daniel Craig. EON had never used the Fleming title The Property of a Lady so they were unlikely to call a Bond film Genoma of a Woman! The title, according to Kontze, was a reference to Swann's DNA. In molecular biology and genetics, a genome is all genetic material of an organism.

August saw Bond 25 finally get a title. You won't be surprised to hear that it wasn't called Genoma of a Woman. Bond 25 was now called No Time to Die. The title was revealed in the Futura Black font. This font has been used for the title sequences of television shows like The Love Boat and Prisoner: Cell Block H and was also used as the wordmark for the National Football League's Minnesota Vikings from 1982 to 2003. No Time to Die was previously the name of a Columbo episode. It was also the alternative British title of a 1958 Cubby Broccoli produced war film called Tank Force! which starred Victor Mature. No Time to Die was the first time the Daniel

Craig era had fallen back on the old Bond trope of using 'die' or 'kill' in the title. The title received a mixed reception. It was pretty generic. No Time to Die sounded a lot like a title thought up by people who couldn't actually think of a title!

No Time to Die felt uninspired as a title but then Bond fans would have plenty of (ahem) time to get used to it before the film came out. The obvious question to consider was whether or not No Time To Die was an improvement over A Reason To Die - which was very nearly chosen as the title of the film. It's purely subjective but you can make a case for A Reason To Die feeling like a more appropriate choice. No Time To Die felt more like a Brosnan title than a Craig era title. EON are clearly never planning to use them, but one could argue that some of the John Gardner (James Bond continuation) novels have better titles than most of the ones EON are coming up with. SeaFire, Scorpius, and Brokenclaw would be decent Bond film titles. A 2017 James Bond comic was called Solstice. Solstice would also be a good future title for a Bond film.

The Daily Mail reported around this time that No Time To Die was the most environmental Bond film ever made. 'Crew members were given reusable water bottles which they filled from taps, saving an estimated 230,000 single-use plastic water bottles. More than 11 tons of packaging waste was also recycled, while producers sent 30 tons of food waste and biodegradable packaging to 'anaerobic digestion', in which micro-organisms break down material, producing a gas that can be used to generate electricity. A further 1.6 tons of food was donated to feed the homeless through the City Harvest charity. Even Bond's beloved gas-guzzling Aston Martin hasn't escaped the green makeover. Craig will drive an electric Rapide E model. Only 155 of the £250,000 vehicles have been built.'

Despite the best efforts of the tabloids to depict Bond 25 as some chaotic and cursed production, the making of the film was alarmingly cheerful and successful. There were no major accidents (aside from part of the 007 sound stage wall being blown off and, thankfully, no one was seriously injured) and the cast and crew were in harmony. Not all Bond productions have been so lucky. Stuntmen have been killed or seriously injured making Bond films. John Glen said in his autobiography that when he directed Licence To Kill the production ended on a bad tempered note with him and Timothy Dalton shouting at each other. When John Glen signed on to direct the film Christopher Columbus: The Discovery a few years later, Dalton, who was slated for the lead, left the project because he didn't want to work with Glen again. Pierce Brosnan later admitted that he did not get on at all with Teri Hatcher when he made Tomorrow Never Dies. Despite his grumpy reputation, there were never any stories that Daniel Craig fell out with a co-star or director. The major problems on Bond 25 occurred prior to production and not during the shoot.

September saw some additional scenes shot in the Faroe Islands. It was also reported that the villain Safin has an island lair and submarine base in the film. The newspapers further reported that Safin had a Zen garden in the film too. Safin has a connection to Madeleine in the film and is seen to giver a mysterious box. Safin is a former Spectre assassin in the story and now a terrorist. Rami Malek said he had his scarred face makeup on when he first met Daniel Craig and Craig was impressed by how 'Bond villain' Malek looked. Malek said that he was impressed by the collaborative way that No Time To Die was made. When they were shooting one particular scene involving Safin and Bond, they didn't feel it was working so changed the dialogue and started it afresh. They even telephoned Phoebe Waller-Bridge so that she could have some input into the changes.

No Time To Die features a time jump after the opening scenes. Cary Fukunaga described the film as one long 'chase' once it kicks into gear. For the PTS where Safin stalks Swann at a frozen lake, Fukunaga drew on horror influences. Although it was sometimes reported that this would be the first PTS not to feature Bond, any 007 worth his salt knew this wasn't really the case. Bond does not appear in the PTS for Live and Let Die nor The Man with the Golden Gun (unless you count a waxwork dummy). Strictly speaking, Bond doesn't appear in the From Russia with Love PTS.

The grand tradition of the PTS featuring a spectacular stunt involving Bond was only really established in 1977's The Spy Who Loved Me when Bond memorably skied off a mountain ledge in a banana yellow ski-suit to evade various gun toting goons. After that it was expected (and hugely anticipated) that each Bond film would begin with a jawdropping stunt sequence. Before the tradition established by The Spy Who loved Me, the pre-title sequences were a little more experimental and unpredictable. Sure, sometimes you got Bond involved in stunts and action (like Goldfinger and Thunderball) but they more licence to do something slightly strange or moody. No Time To Die would mark a return to this tradition.

Lea Seydoux was pictured on the Bond 25 set around this time looking distressed. The media wondered if she was looking distressed in 'character' for the film or whether the French actress had suffered some sort of nervous breakdown on the set! Fortunately it was the former rather than the latter. She was merely acting distressed for scenes in the film. Lashana Lynch was also present during these sequences and wearing military style combat gear. These images were among the most intriguing to be picked up by the media. They related to a story arc that was most definitely marked top secret.

Barbara Broccoli said in an interview at this time that Lashana Lynch would give Bond a run for his money in the film. Lashana Lynch was even given some Tom Ford clothes in line with Bond. It was a rather exhausting production for Lynch as she had to do almost as many action and stunt scenes as Daniel Craig. She said she was having the time of her life though and was loving the chance to be a part of the Bond legacy.

The headaches of the costume department on a Bond film were indicated by the fact there were 33 versions of one of Bond's Tom Ford suits. The different versions were needed for Daniel Craig, his stunt double, stunt drivers, visual effects, and then to depict various stages of wear and tear. Costumes were an expensive part of a Bond film and had to be meticulous and chronologically accurate. Ana de Armas's Michael Lo Lorma Alexandra dress in No Time To Die costs about $1200 in real life but it quickly sold out once images of her wearing the dress were revealed. Chopard supplied the jewellery that Paloma wears with the dress.

The big business of Bond and No Time To Die was illustrated by a Bloomberg breakdown of the extensive product placement deals of Bond 25. There were few companies in the world who wouldn't kill to get their brand in a Bond film. 'There are standard product placements for the likes of Smirnoff vodka and Isabel Marant, Land Rover and Spirit 46 Yachts, Vuarnet, and Anglepoise. And there are more prominent collaborations between the 007 franchise and such brands as Aston Martin, which has become nearly synonymous with James Bond and his cars; and Tom Ford, which has dressed Bond for four consecutive films. No Time to Die will see Bond in Ford clothing for evening wear, suits, shirts, silk accessories, and denim. Ford will also dress the new character Nomi, who is played by Lashana Lynch, with tailor-made jackets, accessories, and eyewear, all handmade in Italy. Meanwhile, many other luxury brands have created their own signature and limited-edition runs of everything from shoes to Champagne.

'GoldenEye Hotel Jamaica has long played an important role in the Bond films, from Dr. No to Live and Let Die. It also provides the opening location for No Time to Die. So the GoldenEye hotel is offering a dedicated package for guests to experience the birthplace of Bond, created by author Ian Fleming after he created GoldenEye. Highlights of the "Ultimate James Bond Experience" include a guided snorkelling tour through Fleming's coral reef and a visit to

Firefly, Noel Coward's former hilltop home. Rates start at $2,630 for four nights starting from now through Dec. 19. Blackwell Jamaican Rum Blackwell, the successful music executive who owns Fleming's former residence noted above, is launching a special 007 Limited Edition release of his eponymous Blackwell Fine Jamaican Rum. The 750 ml bottle is priced at $35; it'll become available in November.

'Adidas will drop the 007 x Adidas No Time to Die collaboration. Little is known about the impending line except that it will include a special edition colorway of the Ultra Boost 20 model that has a solid webbed exterior and a sole insert printed with the names of Bond films through history. Pricing will likely be around $220. "Bolly," as Bond might call it, has been featured in 14 Bond films to date; in honor of No. 25, Bollinger is unveiling an exclusive batch called 007 Special Cuvée. Launched on Oct. 1, just in time for Global James Bond Day, the 007 Special Cuvée comes in special No Time to Die packaging that features images of Craig on the box. It's priced at $85.

'Triumph's Scrambler 1200 appears in several action sequences in the film, so the motorcycle manufacturer's design team collaborated with the Bond stunt team to reconfigure several bikes they're calling the Triumph 1200 Bond Edition. The ride comes painted in Sapphire Black with all-black accents, from the rear mudguard and grab rail to matte black forks, and on to a black powder-coated swingarm and sprocket cover. There's also an oversized Triumph-logo badge on the tank, a brushed decal foil knee pad with hand-painted gold coachline, and the 007 gun branding pressed in the exhaust board and lower side panel finisher. The premium leather seats come with an embroidered logo. Production is limited to 250 models worldwide; pricing starts at £18,500 ($24,022).

'Omega has created the Seamaster Diver 300M James Bond Numbered Edition in Platinum Gold to commemorate the new film. The 42 mm timepiece comes with a black leather strap with platinum stitching and features a platinum-gold plate on the side of the engraved, numbered case. It has 18K white gold indexes, hands, and a Bond family coat-of-of arms set at 12 o'clock; it also has multiple black ceramic elements, a bezel with a platinum diving scale in positive relief, and a black enamel dial in a spiralling gun-barrel design. Elsewhere, a 007 logo is set at 7 o'clock on a white-enamel minute track, and the number 50 is hidden at the 10 o'clock index, itself a reference to the 50th Anniversary of On Her Majesty's Secret Service. Pricing starts at $51,900.

'In the film, the character Q (Ben Whishaw), wears the Swatch Q watch. The stainless steel, 42mm model is part of the Swatch x 007 collection that includes six watches inspired by original movie posters and opening title sequences from Dr. No, On Her Majesty's Secret Service, Moonraker, License To Kill, The World Is Not Enough, and Casino Royale. No Time To Die costume designer Suttirat Anne Larlar designed it in conjunction with Swatch; it comes with a clever case that opens like a laptop with a "screen" and keyboard that paint the letters S W A T C H in red. Production is limited to 7,007 copies worldwide; it costs $220.

'The 141-year-old British staple Crockett & Jones will release a dress shoe tie-in called the 007 Limited Edition James. The shoe is a special version of the Alex model seen in previous Bond films Spectre and Skyfall: simple, slick, "wholecut" design with single high-grade calfskin and leather soles, or, as an option, the rubber Dainite soles that Craig wore during filming. An all-black interior comes with silver foiled Bond logo. The shoes are priced at $1,195 and come with a chrome shoe horn, shoe brush, and a pair of fully lasted, hand-made shoe trees. All are embossed with the 007 logo.

'This 84-year-old British knitwear brand (N.Peal Clothing) launching the 007 cashmere collection of seven classic, yet updated, looks from 50 years of Bond movies. The inspiration comes from such things as a shirt Honey Ryder wore in Dr. No to a V-neck sweater worn by Holly Goodhead in Moonraker. It also includes a Moorland Brown cashmere T-shirt worn by the character Madeleine Swann, and the unisex navy blue, ribbed army sweater worn by Bond in the film (and in its promotional poster). N.Peal had previously worked with the filmmakers on Skyfall and Spectre. Prices start around $350.

'In No Time To Die, Moneypenny (Naomie Harris) carries the MKC x 007 Bond Bancroft satchel. Made in Italy, the leather bag is part of a bigger Kors collection that includes a carryall ($2,350 in calfskin) and a duffel bag ($1,950 in cotton canvas). Orlebar Brown Clothing Each piece in the extensive 007 Heritage Collection from the 13-year-old British clothing brand is inspired by iconic movie scenes, from Harrington jackets to gingham shirts, to linen blazers, and to the "Thunderball Swimshort"—the company's speciality—and the "Dr. No Toweling Polo." Prices start around £95 ($123).'

September saw Daniel Craig interviewed and confirm (yet again) that, yes, this was definitely his last film. He said he had recovered from his injured ankle and that all was going well. Jeffrey wright was also interviewed around this time and said that Felix Leiter plays a pivotal part in the story because it is Felix who lures Bond back into action. The premise of No Time To Die, as revealed by Barbara Broccoli, has Bond sent to retrieve a package but discovering the package is a person. This was not exactly original (the Transporter films with Jason Statham used this plot) but it was a decent McGuffin through which to activate the story. The newspapers reported at this time that the film's plot was about genetic research and that Phoebe Waller-Bridge's main task in her script polish was to make this more understandable to audiences. This story not only depicted Bond fans as idiots but also suggested Phoebe Waller-Bridge was an eminent scientific expert.

Cary Fukunaga said that Daniel Craig changed some of his dialogue on the set of No Time To Die whenever he disliked a line he had been given. It illustrated the power that Craig enjoyed in the franchise - and perhaps too the fairly generous spirit of collaboration that Fukunaga seemed happy to engage with on No Time To Die. You can't really imagine Martin

Campbell or Guy Hamilton being quite so relaxed if a Bond actor had turned up on the set and suddenly started changing all of the dialogue they didn't care too much for. Craig had even been deployed as an emergency writer on Quantum of Solace - although he has happy to admit that he was no Shakespeare. The script was definitely the biggest concern that Bond fans (and perhaps even the producers) had about No Time To Die. They felt sure the concept was fairly solid (in that Bond is retired but drawn back into action by a big mystery that forces him to confront his past) but whether or not the script was sufficiently honed and polished was another matter.

The actual shooting script for No Time To Die was only completed weeks before the film began shooting. Because of all the shenanigans with Danny Boyle and John Hodge leaving the project, there hadn't been a huge amount of time to knock the new screenplay into shape. The selection of Cary Fukunaga as the new director was probably made easier by the fact that he was a writer too. Once he was hired, Fukunaga was able to get to work on the script as fast as he could. The success of No Time To Die as a satisfying film was reliant on Fukunaga's ability to craft a story and screenplay almost as much as it was reliant on Fukunaga's ability in the director's chair.

No Time To Die was the first film in the Bond series to have sequences shot with 65mm IMAX film cameras. 'Filmmaker Cary Joji Fukunaga captured select sequences of No Time to Die using IMAX's extremely high-resolution 15/70mm film cameras to deliver IMAX audiences greater scope and breathtaking image quality,' wrote VitalThrills. 'Only in IMAX theatres will audiences see the film the way it was creatively intended, as the scenes shot with IMAX film cameras will expand vertically to fill the IMAX screen, providing audiences up to 40% more of the image with unprecedented crispness, clarity and color for a truly immersive experience. In addition to being shot with IMAX film cameras and the exclusive expanded aspect ratio, the No Time to Die IMAX release will be digitally re-mastered into the image and sound quality of The IMAX Experience with proprietary IMAX DMR (Digital

Re-mastering) technology. The crystal-clear images, coupled with IMAX's customized theatre geometry and powerful digital audio, create a unique environment that will make audiences feel as if they are in the movie.'

No Time to Die featured a glider sequence as one of its major setpieces. The plane used is a (Fictional Glider) & Boeing C-17A Globemaster III. Bond and Nomi fly the glider out the back of a cargo plane on which Q is naturally aboard. The glider has unfolding wings (as would later be seen in the trailer). This sequence definitely owed something to the Mission Impossible films and with its rather unavoidable use of CGI looked set to be one of the more fantastical sequences to make its way into one of the Daniel Craig films.

The glider sequence was designed to make the experience of No Time To Die feel bigger and more lavish. They wanted audiences to feel like they had full value for money when it came to scope and spectacular stunts.

The glider in No Time To Die is subaquatic and used by Bond and Nomi to get to Safin's lair. A full sized cockpit was built so that Craig and Lynch could be filmed inside - even though CGI would depict the actual flight. The glider was designed to look like a futuristic stealth vehicle. Cary Fukunaga said the glider sequence was an attempt to do something that had never been done in a Bond film before. Bond has fallen out of an aeroplane many times - but never in a glider that could go underwater!

The tabloid silly season when it came to casting the next James Bond continued all through the development and production of No Time To Die. Jamie Bell, James Norton, Michael Fassbender, and Aiden Turner were all at various points anointed as the heir apparent and the favoured son of Barbara Broccoli at different stages of Bond 25's genesis and production. It is certainly true that EON are always on the look out for actors with Bond potential. It would be no surprise if there had been a few sly screen tests during the Craig era or if

Barbara Broccoli had made a mental note (for future reference) of some young British actor she had noticed in something. However, the idea that EON had cast the next Bond while the paint from the Craig era wasn't even dry yet was patently absurd. The next James Bond actor was something that Broccoli didn't even want to think about until such time as it became an absolute necessity.

The concept of the 'reserve Bond', that is to say an actor who is on the EON payroll and ready to step into 007's shoes at the drop of a vodka martini, is something that was real in the Cubby Broccoli era. Michael Billington, a square jawed and hairy chested actor best known for Gerry Anderson's UFO and The Onedin Line, was used by EON to play 007 in screen tests for prospective Bond actresses in the seventies and early eighties. Billington was very nearly cast as Bond in Live and Let Die but lost out to Roger Moore. He was then given a part in the PTS of The Spy Who Loved Me as Sergei Barsov, the lover of Soviet agent Anya Amasova. Billington was more or less an employee of EON and ready to step into 007's shoes at any moment should there be a problem with Roger Moore. Roger and Cubby would usually have some wrangles over Roger's salary for each new film before Roger (usually at the last minute) signed on the dotted line so Cubby liked to have a plan B up his sleeve. Michael Billington was plan B for much of Roger's era.

When they were preparing For Your Eyes Only, Roger Moore's participation was not set in stone so Michael Billington was flown to Corfu (one of the locations for the film) and given a full costume test. In the end though, Roger Moore did the picture and Billington wasn't needed. Billington said that the same thing happened with Octopussy a few years later. Once again, Roger Moore decided to come back and Billington wasn't needed. The late New Zealand actor David Warbeck also claimed that he was something akin to a substitute Bond during the Cubby era. Warbeck, who was a sort of a cult B-movie action and horror star because of the many films he made in Italy, almost became James Bond in the early 1980s when the director John Hough was hired to develop a Bond film. Hough had made a film called Wolfshead (aka Wolfshead: The Legend of Robin Hood) with Warbeck and Cubby Broccoli decided that David Warbeck would be a sensible choice as the new 007 because he knew John Hough. In the end though, Roger Moore, as ever, decided to come back and dashed Warbeck's Bond dream.

The concept of the 'reserve Bond' did not exist in the Barbara Broccoli era. She refused to even contemplate anyone other than Daniel Craig playing Bond and was always willing to wait for as long it took between films for Craig to decide if he wanted to come back or not. There was definitely no plan B in the Barbara Broccoli era. There were rumours that Barbara liked particular actors and kept them in mind (it was alleged a few years ago, for example, that Barbara is quite keen on Jack Huston for Bond) but you can bet your life that none of them were flown to the locations of Daniel Craig films and given a costume fitting. Trying to predict who the next Bond might be is a precarious task because the landscape is always shifting. The next Bond actor could easily be someone why doesn't presently show up on any next 007 list radar.

In September, Liam Gallagher threw his hat into the ring for the No Time To Die Bond theme gig. "The new James Bond one, it's all about dying innit. Die not next week, can't be a***d dying today, might die ******g next month, there's a lot of death going on. But you know they can give us a call, why not." It was probably safe to say that EON were not planning to telephone Liam Gallagher and take him up on his kind expletive filled offer. Dua Lipa and Ed Sheeran were still the favourites with bookmakers and tabloids to sing the theme song. Other new contenders were alleged to be Lewis Capaldi, Ellie Goulding, and James Arthur.

All in all, it was a rather dull and uninspiring list of artists being connected to the theme song. Bond fans could be forgiven for hoping that EON might be able to find someone a little more interesting than the usual tabloid candidates. Harry

Styles was fairly unique in that the tabloids had him as a contender to sing the theme song AND replace Daniel Craig as the next Bond! While it would undoubtedly be a remarkable first for someone to sing the Bond theme and then play James Bond in the next film, the chances of it happening to Mr Styles were pretty slim to say the least.

It was reported in October that Cary Fukunaga had shot three different endings to the film - presumably to wrongfoot any spoiler detectives. It was alleged that they shot all of these endings because they didn't know which one to go for. The 'endings' in question, if they even existed, were clearly not spectacular battle sequences inside a volcano. They were more low-key final shots. The tabloids claimed that it was all so top secret that even Daniel Craig had no idea how the film was going to end. This was somewhat unlikely. Given the creative influence that Craig (who was more or less a producer on the films) had in the series it seemed a rather large stretch to think that he was shooting a film with no idea of how it was going to end. You could probably bet your life that Craig had his two pence when they devised the ending.

The start of October saw the first teaser poster for No Time to Die released. The less said about this amateurish poster the better. It featured a pouting Daniel Craig standing in front of a paint flaked wall. Those who felt the post was rather lacklustre didn't need to worry though. A constant stream of fresh posters for No Time To Die would be endless during the promotional campaigns. There were so many No Time To Die posters in the end that it was almost impossible to keep track of them all.

Pinewood Studios was used to depict Cuba in parts the film. A number of elaborate and impressive Havana street sets were built at Pinewood and used in October as the production neared its end. The Cuban sets took about seven weeks to construct. They were giving an eye-popping amount of colour and lights so that they would look good for scenes set at night. These specific Cuban scenes were supposed to be shot in

Jamaica but Daniel Craig's ankle injury made this impossible and so they had to be delayed and finished off back at Pinewood. The sequences they needed to finish involved a gun battle and chase featuring Bond, Paloma, and various baddies. This sequence, though one of the last things to be shot during production, will take place early in the completed film.

Bond is sent to Cuba by Felix Leiter to retrieve a mysterious package. Felix needs an outsider to do this task because (for obvious political reasons) the CIA are not terribly welcome in Cuba and would only draw attention to themselves. Paloma, a Cuban agent, aids Bond in this mission. Things go awry though when Spectre get involved. Crossing paths with Bond too in Cuba is Nomi - who he previously noticed in Jamaica. The character of Paloma was, as we have noted, a late addition to the script. Ana de Armas said that her character didn't really exist when she was first contacted about taking a part in Bond 25. Phoebe Waller-Bridge was the writer who was instrumental in fleshing out Paloma and putting her into the story. Paloma is required to deploy karate style skills on a number of goons in these sequences.

A few weeks before these last Cuban scenes were shot, Daniel Craig had filmed the scene for what will be the last time we see him in the actual film. This scene was naturally one that no one in the production discussed in the media and swiftly locked away in an EON vault. A few weeks later, Craig was back at Pinewood to shoot his last ever scenes for the production. In the final scene Craig shot for No Time To Die he was, appropriately enough, wearing a tuxedo and disappearing from view in a cloud of smoke. At the conclusion of the final Cuban street scene at Pinewood, it was officially a wrap on No Time To Die. Cary Fukunaga gave a short speech to the crew that had all gathered. There was a round of applause. Daniel Craig gave a speech too but was teary eyed and couldn't remember what he wanted to say. And that was it. The end of an era.

Barbara Broccoli was distraught. It only felt like yesterday when she'd cast Daniel Craig and now it was all over. She couldn't really imagine making a Bond film without her beloved Daniel Craig (although, obviously, this was something she would HAVE to do at some point). Michael G Wilson felt quite sad that shooting was over. It had been an exhilarating ride making No Time To Die. Wilson told the crew that they'd made a 'fantastic' picture. Some of the crew went back to Daniel Craig's trailer and had some cocktails to mark the end of the production. EON officially announced the end of shooting on October the 5th. A special wrap party was held at the Masons' Hall in central London. Daniel Craig then flew home to New York - where he now lives. The next task would be to complete the music score, special effects, ADR (ADR is a process where actors re-record dialogue to improve audio quality or reflect changes), record a theme song, and edit the film. There would then be a massive promotional campaign before No Time To Die was released next April. That was the plan anyway.

* Bond did invent the big budget action franchise but even Cubby Broccoli and Harry Saltzman had their own influences in 1962. The Bond series was heavily influenced by Alfred Hitchcock's masterful 1959 suspense thriller North By Northwest. North By Northwest was in many ways the first James Bond film. It has a suave leading man, adventure, action, varied locations, panache, urbane villains, suggestive humour. The helicopter sequence in From Russia With Love is clearly inspired the cropdusting sequence in North By Northwest. The Bond producers were so inspired by North By Northwest that they even tried to persuade Cary Grant (who was a friend of Cubby Broccoli) to play James Bond in Dr No. Cary Grant, who was in his early sixties at the time, declined this offer though because he felt he was too old for the part.

CHAPTER SIX - BILLIE EILISH

There was a giddy atmosphere now that shooting had ended. The cast scattered in different directions and started to give interviews. Daniel Craig told The Sunday Times that, contrary to his reputation, he wasn't grumpy in real life. Lashana Lynch and Ana de Armas told anyone willing to listen that their characters were far removed from the dated and weak Bond Women of the past and were tough and powerful. Presumably, the No Time To Die women had never heard of Diana Rigg or Honor Blackman. Empire were the quickest out of the blocks to get a No Time to Die story for their magazine and an interview with Barbara Broccoli. Broccoli confirmed (lest any confirmation should be needed) that, once again in the Craig era, things were very 'personal' for Bond in No Time to Die. She told Empire that the villain really gets under Bond's skin in this film. Michael G Wilson was equally bold now that shooting had ended and declared that this would be the best Bond film ever made. He was hardly likely to say anything else was he?

The Daily Mail then ran a story that Barbara Broccoli not only wanted Daniel Craig back for Bond 26 but also wanted him to direct the film too! This article was filed in that (by now) familiar drawer we call 'slow day at the Mail office and in desperate need of some clickbait'. Daniel Craig quickly debunked the Mail story himself when he was asked by a German interviewer if he'd like to direct a Bond film. "For God's sake, no! I want to come home, eat something and then go to bed. If you're a director, then at night you're still with the producers, screenwriters, and on the phone. And then after two hours of sleep, you have to go back up to the set. No thanks!" Craig confirmed once again that, thanks for asking, No Time to Die was definitely the end for him. He must have lost count of how many times he'd been asked that question. This time though he wasn't hedging his bets or playing coy. He gave a direct answer to the question every single time it was asked (and it was asked an awful lot of times).

Scott Z Burns, who seemed to be completely forgotten in the media after Phoebe Waller-Bridge famously had a bash at the script, emerged at this time and discussed his participation in Bond 25. "It's fun for me because a few years ago I got to write a Jason Bourne movie and they're definitely opposite sides of the same coin. So I'm thrilled to have had a chance to contribute to the other side of the coin." However, the writing credits for No Time to Die would list only Neal Purvis, Robert Wade, Cary Fukunaga, and Phoebe Waller-Bridge. Burns was elbowed off the credits list. It appears that No Time To Die's final script used so few of the ideas and lines Burns had created that they didn't feel the need to put him on the credits. Either that or his work was simply going to be uncredited. Burns was probably used to this by now. One of the rules of emergency script doctors is that they don't always get much publicity or attention (because troubled productions tend not to want draw attention to themselves). It's probably not the best job for anyone with a big ego.

This did all illustrate how up in the air the script had been through the genesis and early production of No Time To Die. There were literally four different versions of what Bond 25 could have been floating around. Bond fans could only hope that the version of the film they decided to make in the end would represent the shrewdest choice. This film was ultimately going to be Cary Fukunaga's vision. He would get the roses if it went right and the brickbats if it went wrong. Meanwhile, Daniel Craig appeared on The Late Show and for the millionth time confirmed that this was his last Bond film.

Rami Malek was also starting to do interviews now that production on the film had ended. Of his character he said - "I think you start asking questions about what evil is. And with this character especially I find him fascinating because he can detach from empathy in order to meticulously carry out his will and I start to wrap myself up in who that person is psychologically. He's ruthless and that might be – I'm in danger of giving too much away here – a result of something that's happened to him. but even acknowledging that taps into the analytical side of him as well. I think the fact that he can still find a way to appreciate his own evil is something that is quite petrifying and psychologically something that was not easy for me to tap into."

Naomie Harris was doing interviews too by now and threw herself into the Girl Power spirit of Bond 25. "In Bond 25 you have four strong, intelligent women who are responsible for driving the plot forward. They've never had that in Bond before." Bond fans were understandably weary by now of actresses in the latest film throwing shade on what had gone before and giving the impression that their own part in the next film was revolutionary and awe inspiring. And yet, it so often wasn't. Who was the last truly memorable Bond actress? Since 1969 has any woman in a Bond film ever been as good as Diana Rigg was in On Her Majesty's Secret Service? Has anyone ever been as charismatic as Honor Blackman was in Goldfinger? As iconic as Ursula Andress was in Dr No? For all the criticism of the past from modern actresses when it came to Bond, it was into the past you HAD to travel to find truly memorable and powerful Bond women.

December the 4th saw the release of the first trailer. A hint of Safin, Bond jumping off a bridge, Blofeld back, the Aston Martin, Italy. It actually looked rather a lot like another Sam Mendes film. The return of Christoph Waltz as Blofeld was not exactly a surprise but, a few years previously, the actor had been critical of his own performance in Spectre and suggested he hadn't really done the character justice. EON had not used Blofeld in a Bond film at the time of Spectre since Diamonds Are Forever because the rights to the character were complex and for many years claimed by Kevin McClory. McClory, who died in 2006, was an Irish film producer who worked with Ian Fleming on a screenplay originally called Longitude 78 West - which was proposed to be the first Bond ever film at the time. The film never happened in the end and Broccoli & Saltzman - not Kevin McClory - later launched the Bond film series. However, when Ian Fleming used the Longitude 78 West screenplay for his Thunderball novel without giving McClory (nor any of the other writers who worked on the project) any credit, a court case ensued and Kevin McClory was awarded the legal right to make a film based on Thunderball.

Ian Fleming had been incredibly stupid to write Thunderball without offering any credit to the people who had worked on the story with him. The court case was a great strain and a contributing factor to his early death. Kevin McClory became a great thorn in the side of EON. Even up to his last dying days, he was always threatening to put another 'renegade' Bond film into production. Broccoli and Saltzman, when their Bond series took off, were very shrewd in how they handled McClory. They brought in Kevin McClory as a producer on their own film version of Thunderball. In return for this, McClory agreed not to make a Thunderball film of his own for ten years. Broccoli and Saltzman probably figured that the Bond series wouldn't even be around in ten years. They didn't really care what McClory might do in the far off future.

However, when ten years had passed, the Bond series was still around (in somewhat flagging health after The Man with the Golden Gun but about to get a shot in the arm with The Spy Who Loved Me) and McClory quickly set about making plans for his own Bond film based on his Thunderball rights. He planned to call the film Warhead and brought in Len Deighton and none other than Sean Connery to write the film. Sean Connery (with the possible exception of George Lazenby) is the only Bond actor who would have been disloyal to EON in this way. Connery never felt that he got a fair share of the huge profits his Bond films made in the 1960s and was never shy in expressing his frustration and anger about this. Connery didn't even turn up to Cubby Broccoli's funeral.

Warhead eventually morphed into Never Say Never Again and arrived in 1983. It is a film that many Bond fans felt was disappointing and poorly produced. McClory's biggest coup was persuading Sean Connery to return as Bond in the film. Never Say Never Again was beaten at the box-office that year though by Roger Moore's official Bond film Octopussy. Max Von Sydow played Blofeld in Never Say Never Again but most of his scenes ended up on the cutting room floor. The threat of legal action by Kevin McClory had prevented EON from using Blofeld for decades. A character who seemed an awful lot like

Blofeld was used for a joke in the pre-title sequence of For Your Eyes Only but, this aside, Blofeld had been absent from the official Bond films since we last saw him in Diamonds Are Forever. This meant that Roger Moore, Timothy Dalton, and Pierce Brosnan never tangled with Blofeld in any of their films.

Strangely, the unavailability of Blofeld was not like Sherlock Holmes without Moriarty or Batman without the Joker. Some felt it was probably for the best that Blofeld wasn't in the Bond films anymore. Maybe the days of underground bases and goons in bright boiler suits had gone. This sense was heightened by the Austin powers films - which spoofed sixties spy pop culture and the character of Blofeld. Despite this, 2015's Spectre finally saw the return of Blofeld to the Bond series. The film clumsily attempted to connect Blofeld to the previous Daniel Craig films and, in a bewildering and rather silly twist, revealed that Blofeld was Bond's embittered step-brother. Spectre was proof that EON had no idea what to do with the character of Blofeld in a modern Bond film. It felt like a tremendous waste of a charismatic actor like Waltz. The task of Cary Fukunaga in No Time To Die was to rectify the vague and underwhelming nature of Blofeld in the last film. He simply had to make this famous character more memorable.

The media junket for No Time to Die was cranked up especially early and the cast were soon wheeled out to appear on Good Morning America. Magazine interviews abounded all over the place. Daniel Craig said that the physical battering he took making these films is what made him decide to call it a day. His bones were beginning to 'crack' and he was getting too old for this s*** - to quote Danny Glover in Lethal Weapon. Craig said that his unfortunate comments at the end of the production of Spectre were a result of being tired and sore. He said he virtually made Spectre with a broken leg. Daniel Craig was now nearly as old in real life as Sean Connery had been when he made Never Say Never Again. Never Say Never Again was Connery's first (unofficial of course) Bond film for twelve years and depicted 007 as a retired veteran agent who is pressed back into action. It seemed that No Time

To Die had taken a similar sort of angle when it came to the plot.

In January 2020 it was reported that Dan Romer would no longer be scoring the film and that Hans Zimmer had replaced him. Romer's departure was due to that old chestnut 'creative differences'. His score was apparently deemed too offbeat for the film. For whatever reason, it wasn't quite what they wanted. This was the first time a Bond film had ever changed its composer in post-production and EON did not comment on the departure of Romer. Hans Zimmer needs no introduction. He has scored many films - most famously perhaps the Dark Knight trilogy for Christopher Nolan. Benjamin Wallfisch was apparently in the running to replace Romer too. David Arnold said that no one made any contact with him about replacing Romer.

Zimmer brought in former Smiths guitarist Johnny Marr to work on the music for No Time To Die with him. Hans Zimmer said he had known Barbara Broccoli for many years but he'd never been asked to a Bond film before. He telephoned Johnny Marr to ask if he thought they should do the Bond music together and accept the job and Marr told him they should definitely do the Bond film. It was also confirmed in January that Billie Eilish had been chosen to sing the theme song. This was bad news for Dua Lipa and Ed Sheeran - for so long the favourites according to bookmakers and newspapers. It also put to be bed rumours that Beyonce was going to sing the theme (these rumours had somehow abounded after Beyonce was seen drinking a martini at the Golden Globes).

Billie Eilish had been dropping cryptic Bond themed messages on her social media before the official announcement. Billie Eilish is the youngest artist to write and perform a Bond theme. Billie said of being chosen to sing the new Bond theme - "It feels crazy to be a part of this in every way. To be able to score the theme song to a film that is part of such a legendary series is a huge honour. James Bond is the coolest film franchise ever to exist. I'm still in shock."

Zimmer said that there was a 'box' of potential Bond themes they had to listen to before they picked one and these included a Billie Eilish demo. Zimmer felt that was definitely the right one to choose - although he claimed that EON weren't so convinced at first. Zimmer had never met Billie Eilish before and suggested they fly her over to London to work on the theme. Eilish arrived in Soho suffering from jet lag and was shown some of No Time To Die so that she knew what sort of mood the film was going through. You'd think though that if she'd watched any of the previous Craig films she'd already have had a good idea about that! No Time To Die was business as usual really for the Craig films. It wasn't going to be a radical departure in terms of mood.

Cary Fukunaga said that he had championed Billie Eilish for the theme song and had to persuade the producers it was a good idea. They didn't seem to know who Billie Eilish was. You could probably forgive Michael G Wilson and even Barbara Broccoli if they weren't totally up to speed on the latest teenage music sensation. Daniel Craig, who seemed to have a personal veto on music artists, was another of the Bond team who was a bit foggy on Billie Eilish before Fukunaga threw her hat into the mix. "What I was mostly involved with was trying to get Billie in front of Barbara and Daniel, who were less aware of Billie's growing popularity," said Fukunaga. "I was really vying for them as a choice that wouldn't be so predictable. I thought it (the song) was chilling when I first heard it. After that, it was really just trying to shape it to have the bigger scale of a Bond song. But really, all the bones were already there. Hans himself said, 'I don't have to do a whole lot, this song is fantastic."

Billie's full name is Billie Eilish Pirate Baird O'Connell. She was born in December 18, 2001, in Los Angeles. Billie is part of what is known as Generation Z - those born between 1997 and 2012. Billie was raised in Highland Park, a neighborhood about thirty minutes from The Graceland Inn, West Hollywood. Billie's brother Finneas is a singer, songwriter, record producer, musician, and actor. He has been instrumental in Billie's career. Billie's songs have been described as explorations of loneliness, dreams, anxiety, and alternative perspectives. Billie is the youngest female artist ever to have a number one album in Britain. Billie says that her synesthesia (a condition in which people relate to concepts and objects in colours) is a big influence on the way that she creates songs. "I think visually first with everything I do, and also I have synesthesia, so everything that I make I'm already thinking of what colour it is, and what texture it is, and what day of the week it is, and what number it is, and what shape. We both have it [she and brother Finneas], so we think about everything this way."

Billie was only fifteen when her debut EP, Don't Smile At Me, was released. John Janick, the chief executive of Interscope Records, said of Billie - "Her sense of style, how she thinks, the way she talks – everything about her was just different. She had such a strong point of view, especially for being 14 years old." Billie said that watching Runaway by Aurora on YouTube was a big inspiration when it came to her musical career. Billie says she never bought a music CD because she grew-up in the streaming age. Billie is the youngest artist to ever get listed in the BBC Radio 1 Sound Polls.

The origin of her breakthrough song Ocean Eyes is that Billie's dance teacher wanted a song to use to create a new dance routine. Finneas had written the song Ocean Eyes for his own band and decided to perform it with Billie so it could be used for the dance. Ocean Eyes became a huge hit when it was put on SoundCloud. Ocean Eyes was certified platinum by the RIAA. Billie says of the amazing and unexpected success of Ocean Eyes - "We put it on SoundCloud with a free download link next to it so my dance teacher could access it. We had no intentions for it, really. But basically overnight a ton of people started hearing it and sharing it. Hillydilly, a music discovery website, found it and posted it and it just got bigger and bigger. It was really surreal. Then, Danny Ruckasin, who is now my manager, reached out to my brother and was like, "dude, this is going to get huge and I think you're going to need help along the way. I want to help you guys." We were like, "that's swag!"" On Billie's Youtube channel, the Ocean Eyes video has been viewed 260 million times.

Billie released her EP 'Don't Smile At Me' on August 11, 2017, at the age of fifteen. In 2019, Billie was crowned the Billboard Woman of the Year. Billie earned her first Grammy Award nominations at the 62nd annual ceremony, where she was nominated for Best New Artist. At just seventeen, Billie became the youngest artist to be nominated in all 'big four' Grammy categories. The songs featured on Billie's debut album were streamed 194 million times in the first full week they were available. Of the songs on Don't Smile at Me, four went Gold and one went Platinum. Billie Eilish's debut album When We All Fall Asleep, Where Do We Go? smashed vinyl record sales upon its release. When We Fall Asleep Where Do We Go had more than 15 billion worldwide streams. Billie won on five of the six awards she was nominated for at the 2020 Grammy Awards.

Billie Eilish is the youngest person ever to win album of the year at the Grammys. When Billie played the Reading Festival in 2019, she attracted one of the biggest crowds ever witnessed at the event. 'What a show we just witnessed,' wrote the festival website. 'Billie Eilish gave us a Main Stage performance that we'll never forget. As soon as her infamous intro track began to play out, floods of fans could be seen running across the field to catch a glimpse of one of the most famous teenagers in the world right now.' Billie was the first 'international' artist to be awarded a Breakthrough Award at the Brits.

When We All Fall Asleep Where Do We Go? had the biggest opening week for a debut album in the history of Billboard's current chart. 'Everything I Wanted' enabled Billie to tie the record for the most number one songs by a solo artist on Billboard's alternative songs chart. Billie's 49-date Where Do We Go? world tour sold 500,000 tickets in North America,

South America, and Europe within an hour of its announcement. The audio of Copycat has over one hundred million views on Billie's YouTube channel. When Billie's album When We All Fall Asleep Where Do We Go? debuted at number one, she became the youngest artist to do this since Demi Lovato released Here We Go Again aged 16 back in 2009. On Billie's Youtube channel, the Bury A Friend video has been viewed nearly 340 million times. On Billie's Youtube channel, When the Party's Over has been viewed 530 million times.

Billie was the seventh most viewed female artist on YouTube in 2019. The number one spot went to Cardi B. A study by the Institute of Contemporary Music Performance in 2019 concluded that Billie Eilish was the hardest working female artist in music. The study said Billie had played 184 shows across 23 countries from January 2018 to August 2019. My Boy sold a certified 200,000 units in Britain. According to Bloomberg's latest Pop Star Power Rankings, Billie Eilish is the seventh biggest music star in the world. Billie says she suffered from Body dysmorphic disorder the most when she was in a competitive dance company as a child. "I was always worried about my appearance. That was the peak of my body dysmorphia. I couldn't look in the mirror at all. I've never felt comfortable in really tiny clothes." Billie's style has been described as androgynous. She eschews the 'girly' fashion style of artists like Ariana Grande. Billie has joked that her clothes are always "eight-hundred times too big" for her.

Billie has appeared on the cover of Hot Press, Grazia, Sound on Sound, and Stellar amongst many others. Billie has also been on the cover of Rolling Stone. Billie was ranked number one in 'celebrity style searches' on Google in 2019. Number two was the late icon Audrey Hepburn. Unlike some other singers, Billie does not think of her onstage persona as an alter-ego or character she has created. She thinks she is pretty much the same person all the time. A number of music writers have compared Billie Eilish to Kate Bush - an eccentric and enigmatic British singer who first became famous in the 1970s.

The most obvious similarities are that Kate Bush was also a teenage prodigy who had her family working with her.

When Billie performed at the Leeds Festival in 2019, ticket demand was so great that she was moved to the main stage. Bad Guy was the most streamed song of 2019. When We All Fall Asleep Where Do We Go? was certified double Platinum in America and Canada. Billie won three categories at the 2019 Mexican Telehit Awards. Billie also won two AMAs by the age of seventeen. Billie performed to 40,000 people at Glastonbury. She had to be moved to a bigger stage at Glastonbury because so many people wanted to see her. Cassette tapes, long considered a defunct technology (and accounting for only 0.2% of the albums market), increased their sales by 112% in Britain in 2018. Billie Eilish was cited as the main reason for this. Walkmans and cassette tapes had apparently become trendy again in a retro nostalgia sort of way. When We All Fall Asleep Where Do We Go? was the highest selling cassette tape in Britain for 2018. Billie is only the ninth artist to reach 10 or more weeks at number one on Billboard's Artist 100. In 2019, Billie was nominated for nine MTV Video Music Awards. Billie is only the fourth female artist ever to win a Gramy for album of the year with a debut album. Bad Guy reached number one in more than a dozen countries.

Billie much prefers to write songs with her brother Finneas than producers or songwriters outside the family. She has a form of musical 'shorthand' with Finneas where they both know what their strengths are - something which obviously makes the songwriting process more productive and less time consuming. Billie says that one of the big advantages of working with Finneas is that they are both completely honest with each another. If they think a song isn't working they will openly express this to one another. This works as an editing process and means that they never release a song that one of them is unhappy about or felt could have been done better than it was. Billie was the first artist born in the 2000's to have a number one album. Billie says her critics often say that she whispers rather than sings. Billie's music has been described as 'genre bending' in that it doesn't neatly fit into any specific category.

Billie wrote her first song when she was only four years old. The Ranker website voted Billie Eilish the second most famous singer in the world in 2020. The number one spot went to Ariana Grande. As of 2020, Billie has 62 million followers on Instagram. Billie Eilish has nearly 30 million subscribers to her YouTube channel. Dave Grohl raved about Billie when he saw her in concert for the first time. "I went to see Billie Eilish not too long ago. Oh my god man. Unbelievable. My daughters are obsessed with Billy Eilish. And what I'm seeing happening with my daughters is the same revolution that happened to me at their age. My daughters are listening to Billie Eilish and they're becoming themselves through her music. She totally connects to them. So we went to go see her play at the Wiltern, and the connection that she has with her audience is the same thing that was happening with Nirvana in 1991. The people in the audience knew every word. And it was like our little secret. So I don't know...and her music is hard to define! I don't know what you call it! I try to describe her to people and I don't know... I don't even know what to call it. But it's authentic. And I would call that rock n roll. So.... I don't care what sort of instruments you use to do it. When I look at someone like Billie Eilish, I'm like...man....rock n roll is not even close to being dead..."

No Time To Die became Billie's first number one single in the UK. Billie and Finneas said that their James Bond theme took only three days to write. They said they listened to past Bond themes in preparation for crafting the song. No Time To Die peaked at number 16 on the Billboard Hot 100. Billie and Finneas completed their Bond them with the film's composer Hans Zimmer and Johnny Marr. Hans Zimmer said there were several people in the running for the Bond song before they chose Billie. Johnny Marr said he thought it was a good idea to pick Billie for the Bond theme. "Before I'd even heard the song, I thought it was just a smart idea and this was before all the Grammys and stuff. When I heard the song, I thought 'this is fantastic'. It's very brave, being very minimalist. It's her sound, and then the trick was to Bond-ify it. It was already a great song, but from a sound point of view, to Bond-ify it without doing the obvious. It's really easy to be bombastic, so it was a case of less is more, and making it work with the film."

The audio for No Time To Die has had over seventy million 'views' on Billie's YouTube channel. Johnny Marr said - "Billie's just the best new, I don't wanna say pop act, but it's great when someone that cool is that popular, individual and a lot of people can relate to her. She's a really good musician, and her family is a really musical family, very soulful. I know a great musician when I see one." Of the Bond theme, Finneas O'Connell said - "Well, at the risk of saying something that hopefully I'm allowed to say — hopefully this won't be a long bleep-out thing. We were not really 'approached' about it. We fought it out for a year. We've always wanted to write a James Bond theme song. And you know, it's a legendary franchise, so we had to convince a lot of people that we were the right choice. And then we had to write a song that everybody liked. So it was a hard-won process. But everybody that we worked with on it, Barbara Broccoli, the producer of the Bond franchise (alongside Michael G Wilson), we got to work with Hans Zimmer and Steven Lipson in the studio — it was a real joy."

The Chicago Tribune didn't seem to like Billie's Bond song very much. 'No Time To Die is a quavering, drab thing that doesn't have tension, or life, or drama, or pretty much anything interesting, right down to the utterly ordinary arrangement better suited for a wine commercial. A theme is supposed to be more than incidental music that burbles innocently in the background. There is the swell of percussion and string drama near the end but it's a false start, because the artist singing the tune isn't capable of rising to the occasion. Eilish's vocal range moves from whisper to coo, veering from that only for an instant, just at the end, which makes it clear why she sticks to that range. Look, who's going to say no to that kind of assignment, right? You get a global single without having to do much except, in the case of Eilish, mutter into a microphone.' The BBC's Mark savage offered a more generous verdict - 'The musician is known for her intimate, designed-for-headphone vocal style, but she rises to the challenge of the song's soaring climax, with her early vulnerability transforming into strength and resolve. It's easily the most audacious and atmospheric take on the Bond theme in recent memory.'

The commercial success of the Billie Elish theme song justified the decision to select her as the theme artist. That's really how the Bond themes work these days. The main goal is to hire someone who is currently very popular and if they come up with a decent song then that's a bonus. Having the best prospective Bond theme song doesn't mean you will get chosen. The k.d. lang song Surrender for Tomorrow Never Dies is vastly superior (and much more Bondian) than Sheryl Crow's forgettable title theme but Surrender ended up on the end credits. Sheryl Crow was chosen because someone obviously decided she was a bigger star and would sell more records. Forever - I Am All Yours by Eva Almér was a fantastic proposed theme song for Quantum of Solace but the truly atrocious Another Way to Die (surely the worst Bond theme of all time) by Jack White and Alicia Keys was chosen instead.

It is open to debate if Billie Eilish and her brother did actually come up with a good Bond theme for No Time To Die. Critics of Billie Eilish (who are decidedly in the minority because she is, as we have just seen, hugely popular) would contend that she whispers her vocals rather than sings. No Time To Die sounds like it was recorded in an airing cupboard. The last Bond theme by Sam Smith for Spectre was also a mumbling mournful sort of song that didn't really stay in the memory. You would hardly call these low-key introspective Bond songs ear worms! Bond fans who would like something a little more upbeat for a change could be forgiven for having this desire. Still, you can't argue with the figures. By any standards, Billie's Bond theme was a big hit in unit sales and gave the film plenty of welcome publicity.

CHAPTER SEVEN - THE WAITING GAME

In January a number of reports (gleaned from running times listed by foreign distributors) indicated that No Time to Die would be nearly three hours long. Three hours! That was Lord of the Rings territory. Bond writers Purvis & Wade commented on this story though. They'd seen a rough cut of the film and said the version they watched wasn't three hours long. Ben Whishaw was interviewed in January and said that No Time to Die draws a line under the Craig films and wraps things up. This really was the end of an era. Ben Whishaw said he never did get a full script for No Time To Die so he didn't really know yet what happens in the rest of the film. He only got the script parts for his scenes - which were not shot in chronological order. Whishaw said that even if he did know what happened in the film he obviously wouldn't be allowed to divulge any details anyway.

Whishaw said his contract on the Bond films had now expired and he might never play Q again. Who knew what would happen in the next film? Whishaw had no idea if they'd ever ask him back again. Would they cast a new M, Q, and Moneypenny once there was a new Bond actor? No one had the faintest idea. These were decisions for the future. For now, the Bond team were simply concentrating on making No Time To Die a success and right now that meant putting everything they had into the massive promotional campaign.

Ben Whishaw said that Cary Fukunaga worked in an improvisational way and was always willing to change something if he didn't feel a scene was working to his satisfaction. The interview revealed that there was a tight deadline when they made No Time To Die. The cast were impressed at the way Cary Fukunaga was able to get the film finished on time and maintain a friendly and relaxed atmosphere on the set. Barbara Broccoli and Michael G Wilson were so impressed by Cary Fukunaga that they said they'd have no hesitation in working with him again in the future. Fukunaga seemed open to this and said in an interview that it would be fun to come back to the franchise and make a movie with the next Bond actor.

Marketing is definitely something that the modern Bond films are very good at. Timothy Dalton's last Bond film Licence To Kill was severely hamstrung by a penny pinching marketing campaign (which Cubby Broccoli complained about) by MGM that jettisoned a spectacular art campaign for some very shoddy and cheap posters for North America. The marketing on the Brosnan and Craig films though has been excellent. When a Bond film is released today you would literally have to be living on another planet not to notice the marketing and promotional campaign. No stone is left unturned in the quest to inform audiences that Bond is back. One very shrewd thing the Bond franchise did after Dalton era was move the release dates of the films to the winter rather than the summer. This has generally meant that Bond films will now open at a time when there is less competition at the box-office. It isn't always this simple (Tomorrow Never Dies found itself up against James Cameron's Titanic - but then who would have guessed that Titanic would be so insanely popular and make two billion dollars?) but, for the most part, opening Bond films around October or November has been a profitable strategy and new tradition.

On February the 2nd, 2020, a 30-second spot for No Time to Die ran late in the second quarter of the Super Bowl. Commercials for the Super Bowl cost more than $5 million each for 30 seconds. The No Time To Die Super Bowl spot threw in some of the glider sequence featuring Bond and Nomi. The trailers for No Time To Die showcased, as you would expect, plenty of action (in particular the bike and Aston Martin chase) but also revealed that Bond and Madeleine seemed to have become estranged since the events of Spectre. There was a hint in the trailers that Bond felt betrayed by her. The trailers were proof, should we need it, that the 'personal' nature of the Craig films was set to continue. If you liked this approach then you were going to like No Time To Die. If you didn't like this approach then tough luck. You'd just have to hope the next era of Bond would be more to your taste.

The promotional campaign for No Time To Die started almost as soon as the film had finished shooting and showed no sign of letting up. MGM and EON were going all in to make No Time To Die as big a blockbuster as they possibly could. It was reported though in February that the promotional campaign for No Time to Die had been suspended in China because of fears over the coronavirus. This was merely the first inkling of the trouble to come. The world outside of China was not yet aware that this virus was going to have profound and worrying consequences for everyone - even James Bond.

'Due to the coronavirus epidemic,' reported Variety, 'the new James Bond film No Time to Die has cancelled its Beijing premiere as well as a promotional tour with talent in April, according to Chinese reports. The film, which marks star Daniel Craig's last turn as the iconic spy, is set to debut in North America on April 10. Chinese cinemas and huge swathes of the world's second largest economy have been shut since the country's lunar new year holiday last month. Even if theaters reopen in April in time for the film to screen, Chinese fans will be unable to catch Craig and the film's other stars in the flesh, as they have been advised to stay out of the country at that time, a Chinese report said. The coronavirus, which first appeared in China's Hubei province, has now infected more than 71,000 people globally and killed 1,775, including five people outside of mainland China.

'The releases for all Valentine's Day films in China and most of its other February titles have been cancelled, with no end in sight for cinema closures as citizens across the country remain in enforced self-quarantine, rarely venturing outside their homes. China is one of the most important overseas markets for the Bond franchise, and was the highest grossing overseas territory for its last installment, Spectre, other than the U.K. That film, also starring Craig, made $881 million worldwide, $84 million of which came from China. Craig recently appeared in the murder mystery Knives Out, which was released in China in November and went on to gross $28 million in the country. This far outstripped its haul in all other territories, including the U.K., where it made $17 million.' One could see the importance of the Chinese market with those figures. $84 million alone for Spectre in Chinese cinemas. An Imax poster for No Time To Die was released at the end of Febuary as Omega continued to ramp up their own campaign. No Time to Die was now merely weeks away from release. Michael G Wilson suggested in an interview that the pre-title sequence would be twenty minutes long. Was he serious? That couldn't be right! Another poster was released before the end of the month. Ana de Armas didn't make it onto the list of credits at the bottom of the latest poster - which confirmed her role was minor. Ana de Armas was being used extensively in the marketing campaign though. It was then reported that coronavirus was responsible for the cancellation of the No Time To Die promotional tour and premieres in Japan and South Korea. This was further evidence that big trouble was brewing not just for James Bond but other productions and the cinema industry in general. Bond is a very international franchise. It needed those international markets. The news from China, South Korea, and Japan was worrying for MGM and EON. However, there was still hope and optimism. At this stage no one seemed to suspect how bad things were about to get for the movie industry.

Bond fans in Britain began buying their cinema tickets for No Time to Die. Posters for the film were plastered over buses and advertised in local cinemas everywhere. A big celebrity premiere was planned for the Royal Albert Hall. The film was almost here. No Time to Die was projected to earn between $75-100 million in its first three days in the United States. A huge box-office was expected. Bond films usually opened around November (at least they had done ever since the franchise returned after a hiatus with GoldenEye in 1995) but No Time To Die was going to open in April. The competition it was expected to face was minimal - The New Mutants, Trolls World Tour, and Antlers. MGM must have been dreaming of doing Skyfall numbers all over again. The running time was now alleged to be 163 minutes. This was a slight concern for MGM because such a long film meant that fewer screenings could be squeezed in. Generally though, despite the news coming out of China, EON and MGM were increasingly full of optimism. No Time To Die was finally here and it was going to make a gigantic sum of money. More posters abounded. Billie Eilish went to number one. Things were looking good.

Then it all went wrong for MGM and EON. The coronavirus was starting to become bigger news. We were all, wherever we lived in the world, beginning to realise that this was going to affect all of us - not just China and its neighbours. Unfortunately for No Time To Die, this was the first major film set for release since the coronavirus outbreak. In many ways, Bond was now a test case for what would happen if you tried to open a big film worldwide in this current climate. Other studios who had their own big films to release in 2020 were watching very closely to see what would happen to No Time To Die.

Speculation over whether or not No Time to Die should be delayed and not released at all began to gain traction in the media and on Bond forums. Around this time major sporting and entertainment events were starting to be cancelled. We were beginning to deduce that it might be a good idea, for own health and to contain the virus, to avoid crowds and other people. Cinemas were closed in China and Japan. The United States and Europe were beginning to experience the first signs of what was projected to be an epidemic. The idea of releasing a major film into cinemas in April with this escalatingly grim backdrop was starting to look insane.

The James Bond fan website MI6 published an editorial on

their front page in which they argued for the film to be delayed. The editorial (laughably in hindsight) suggested the film should be moved back a couple of months to the summer when the virus would be 'under control'. This illustrated just how little anyone knew at the time of both the virus and the profound economic danger it posed to the cinema industry. At the start of March, the inevitable happened when James Bond twitter announced that No Time To Die had been officially delayed and would no longer open in April. 'MGM, Universal and Bond producers, Michael G Wilson and Barbara Broccoli, announced today that after careful consideration and thorough evaluation of the global theatrical marketplace, the release of NO TIME TO DIE will be postponed until November 2020.' The postponement of the film had become unavoidable by the time that the announcement was made.

At the start of March, Daniel Craig was required to go ahead with his pre-booked appearance on Saturday Night Live as the guest host. It was a fairly bizarre situation now as the No Time to Die promotional campaign was still flailing around like a giant out of control prehistoric monster but the actual film had been delayed by several months and wasn't actually going to be released yet. Also in March, in an interview for GQ, Daniel Craig confirmed that, for the billionth time, this was definitely his last Bond film. This was the right time to walk away and embrace some new acting challenges. Craig, who wasn't getting any younger, felt that he'd taken enough punishment making the Bond films and now was the right time to bow out and pass the baton on to a new actor.

Daniel Craig said he had (some time ago now) seen a rough cut of No Time To Die in Soho and was happy with how it had turned out. Craig said he decided to watch the film alone so that he could absorb it fully and concentrate. There was no music score and the special effects hadn't been finished but Craig felt the film worked. He thought it was good.

Although he now lived in New York, Craig had to fly to London to get his special private screening of No Time To Die. Lea

Seydoux also said in an interview she had watched the film and that it made her cry. Seydoux, in a later interview, said that her character was an 'interesting woman' - the likes of which has been absent in previous Bond films. Diana Rigg as Tracy di Vicenzo must have been extremely uninteresting then according to the logic of Lea Seydoux.

There were naturally fears now that No Time to Die might be pirated or spoiled before it could released. The decision to delay the film ultimately came as a consequence of Bond's reliance on international markets. MGM wanted the movie to have a wide release (as opposed to releasing it at a time when cinemas in some countries were closed). The desire was for everyone to be able to enjoy the film at the same time. It was a cruel blow for Bond fans who had already waited five years for a new film but everyone understood the situation. Now that the coronavirus was receiving more news coverage and affecting all of us, no one had any desire to sit in a cinema full of strangers. The risk was too great to take a gamble. A number of countries were also putting in place lockdowns and closing cinemas anyway.

In March, a YouTube channel called Midnight's Edge claimed that No Time To Die was about to undertake some reshoots to change a couple of key scenes. Midnight's Edge bills itself as a look at the production of film and TV but without the 'spin'. They post a lot of videos about behind the scenes trouble and casting. Some of this stuff is unverified gossip though and not always accurate. The website claimed - "Approval for two reshoots has been given the go ahead for next week. These moves are to change plot beats that tested poorly with audiences. Those plot beats in question were pertaining to a global viral outbreak. Something that was believed to hit a little too close to home with the current pandemic that the world still finds itself in the grips of." Midnight's Edge claimed that test screenings for the film had not gone very well. This was contrary to the Daily Mail's Baz Bamigboye - who claimed that he'd heard good things about No Time To Die from those that had seen it.

The British newspapers picked up on the Midnight's Edge story and regurgitated it as though it were fact. There was though no verifiable truth in the story. The cast and crew were not getting back together for expensive reshoots and the story about negative test screenings was pure speculation. No Time To Die was locked and finished. This wasn't Justice League. A different version of the film wasn't now being secretly shot at Pinewood. As for the plot featuring elements that might be too sensitive now in light of all too real and tragic health fears in the world, this was also purely speculative. No Time To Die was not undergoing extensive reshoots. The test screenings, whatever the results may have been, were not really important now anyway. The film would have been edited and completed after those screenings were taken into account. All that really mattered now was how Bond fans and casual audiences reacted to the film when they finally got a chance to see it.

Cary Fukunaga said around this time that he was completely finished with his work on No Time to Die and was not tempted to 'tinker' with the film during the delay. He was happy with the film and it would now stay under lock and key until such time as it could be safely released in cinemas. "I don't think anyone could have foreseen how the world came to a complete standstill, but I did think audiences would not be going to cinemas. You could just fiddle and tweak and it doesn't necessarily get better. For all intents and purposes, we had finished the film. I had mentally finished the film. Mentally and emotionally." Cary Fukunaga said he hadn't seen all of the Bond films before No Time to Die and only became a fan because of Casino Royale. Interestingly, Fukunaga said the first Bond film he remembered watching as a child was A View To a Kill. "The first Bond I ever saw was A View To A Kill, with Roger Moore. The whole finale took place in the Bay Area which is where I'm from. So to see my home on the big screen was really exciting. It made your own life seem larger than itself."

Cary Fukunaga said in a new interview that the look of No

Time To Die had been designed as if it takes place in twilight. He wanted a moody sort of ambiance. Fukunaga said that his biggest influence was Casino Royale - which he felt was vastly superior to the three Craig films that followed. Another influence was On Her Majesty's Secret Service. Fukunaga said he felt a particular pressure with this film because he was also responsible for the plot and screenplay. If people didn't think the story in this film worked then he would obviously end up taking the lion's share of the blame for that.

June 2020 saw the first potential spoiler alerts for No Time To Die when it was revealed that a little girl named Mathilde will feature in the film. The character, played by Lisa-Dorah Sonne, was alleged to be the daughter of Bond and Madeleine Swann. However, it was then alleged that Mathilde was a clone of Swann created by Safin. The reveal was instigated by call sheets for No Time To Die which were put up for sale on ebay. The Sun newspaper put 2 and 2 together and came up with 967. They declared that EON were now preparing to launch a spin-off franchise where Bond trains Mathilde to become a deadly assassin!

The scenes with Mathilde were shot in Italy (which doubled for Safin's submarine base) in September 2019. These scenes were the ones that EON were most eager to keep secret. Mathilde might be inspired by elements of You Only Live Twice - where Kissy becomes pregnant. These scenes form part of the extended epilogue for No Time To Die. The epilogue is the reason why the film is so long. The concept of Bond ending No Time To Die with a five year-old daughter was not one that seemed to go down terribly well. Even Britt Eklund complained that it would ruin the mystique of Bond. It would be another of the soap operish elements that have dogged the Daniel Craig films. In her press interviews, Naomie Harris had said that Bond fans would be absolutely shocked by some of the twists in No Time To Die. Mathilde was clearly very much on her mind when she made these comments.

There were a seemingly endless stream of No Time To Die

features in magazines throughout 2020. There was a danger of revealing too much but the cast and crew were shrewd enough not to fall into this trap and managed to keep the secrets of the film up their sleeve. The main danger was that Bond fans might get sick to death of No Time To Die after almost a year of endless promotion and magazine and website features. The interviews were often done months ago in anticipation of the April release. There was nothing much EON and MGM could do. They couldn't order the magazines and websites to keep their Bond exclusives on ice until such time as the film might be released. At the very least though, this drip feed of No Time To Die features was good publicity and keeping the film's profile consistently high.

It must have been a strange situation for Daniel Craig - for whom the promotional campaign for No Time To Die was originally supposed to be a short farewell tour. Craig had made it clear he was done with the part but until such time as No Time To Die was released and a new actor was cast he was still James Bond. Craig could be forgiven for feeling a little weary at the prospect of possibly having to do a fresh batch of interviews for the new release date. If it was a strange situation for Daniel Craig, it was also a strange situation for Cary Fukunaga. Fukunaga said it was weird to complete a film but then not know when it could be released. He must have felt like Terry Gilliam after he'd made Brazil. If was only when people were able to watch the film and offer some reviews and opinions that Fukunaga would really know if No Time To Die was a success or not. The film was in a strange limbo until then.

No Time to Die hadn't even reached its next projected release date when the Bond silly season began again in earnest. A number of newspapers latched onto an unverified website report that Tom Hardy had signed a deal to replace Daniel Craig and would be unveiled as the new 007 at the end of 2020. Putting aside the fact that, at 43, Hardy was plainly on the old side to be kickstarting the next era of Bond (at the rate EON make films, Hardy would have been an old age pensioner by the time he got to his third adventure!), it was surely unrealistic to believe that EON had cast the new Bond before the last film featuring the old Bond had even come out!

Still, if nothing else, the Tom Hardy story proved that the search for the next Bond is one of those games we never tire of. Many years from now the story of how EON found Daniel Craig's replacement will be told and what a tale it will be. Pop stars who have never so much as acted in a school play will be erroneously put on the candidate shortlist by tabloids. Actors who played bad tempered bearded small businessmen in Emmerdale and Hollyoaks will regale us with tales of how they read for the part and got really (honestly) close to being picked. A man with no IMDB credits to his name aside from Megacrocogoldfish v Giantoctopus will tell us on his website that he got to the final four and bumped into Aiden Turner in the toilets at Pinewood Studios. That was the future though. There was still a small matter of No Time To Die before the dust could finally settle on the Daniel Craig era.

The first film to have a stab at a cinema release in these unprecedented times had been Christopher Nolan's Tenet. You wouldn't called Tenet a tentpole blockbuster - although with a budget of $200 million it was the biggest film Nolan had made. Tenet wasn't Star Wars though or even Bond for that matter. Tenet's American box-office was fairly dismal but it made (at the time of writing) $283.4 million in other territories. James Bond was clearly a more commercial prospect than Tenet. There were enough flickers of hope for the bean counters to believe that releasing No Time to Die in November might be a gamble worth taking. Cinema chains in particular were desperate and banking on No Time to Die to save them from oblivion. So another promotional campaign for the movie was launched. Brands hocked their No Time to Die tie-ins. Daniel Craig was booked for chat shows. Barbara Broccoli released a podcast (which sounded a lot like something that was probably recorded for a DVD commentary).

In August it was silly season time again for the newspapers when it was reported that former Batman star Ben Affleck, who was the real life boyfriend of Ana de Armas, had been banned from attending the No Time To Die premiere lest he should overshadow the event. According to CinemaBlend - 'Over the weekend, a rumour began running around that Hollywood it couple Ben Affleck and Ana de Armas might have hit a minor snafu. Namely, an unnamed source mentioned that with movies starting to gear back up, Affleck may not be welcome at the No Time To Die premiere. Yes, I'm talking about the new 25th flashy James Bond movie starring Daniel Craig and featuring Ana de Armas. The Sun newspaper reported (via NZ Herald) a source in Los Angeles saying that Ben Affleck could "overshadow" the whole event. The source called Affleck showing up "a disaster," mentioned the couple's penchant for "mushy PDAs" and said if her new beau showed it would be "overshadowing the event."

'Apparently, the powers that be want to avoid "a circus sideshow" and keep the focus on Bond, but can you imagine how awkward that conversation could be with Ana de Armas? It's true that No Time To Die will be a big event movie for the Bond franchise. It is Daniel Craig's last outing in the role and while Ana de Armas is currently a popular actress and a splashy get for that franchise, her PDA with Ben Affleck theoretically could overshadow what should be the news story: the end of a Bond era. It's also worth noting that Ben Affleck and Ana de Armas' burgeoning relationship has been one of the major focal points in entertainment news since the start of the pandemic. So, thinking people might care most about their PDA and romance isn't as far-fetched of a rumour as it may at first seem.'

Another strange poster was released in September. It made Daniel Craig look like he was sitting on the toilet. An action packed trailer was then released with explosions, stunts, and more glimpses of Safin's submarine base - which was clearly inspired by The Spy Who Loved Me. Another poster was released - this time of Daniel Craig with a machine gun. Guns used by the characters in No Time To Die are the Walther PPK, SIG Sauer P226R, FN Browning Hi-Power, Heckler and Koch MP7A1, AKS-74U, CSA Sa vz. 58 Compact, Mk 18 Mod 0, and Beretta ARX-160 A3. A music video for the Billie Eilish theme was released - a low-key black and white affair with Billie singing against a darkened backdrop as a few clips from the film occasionally played out in the background. Film magazines had yet more interviews with the cast and crew and more behind the scenes photographs. This time, finally, No Time to Die looked like it was going to see the light of day. And then, as before, the plug was pulled at the last minute.

The second postponement of the film, like the first, was announced only weeks before it was due to be released. No Time to Die, back in April 2020, had been the first major release to be affected by the Covid virus. A number of films thereafter simply decided to bypass cinemas and go straight to VOD and streaming. This though was not really an option if you'd just spent north of $200 million on Wonder Woman or a Bond film. None of the big films of 2020 wanted to be the first test case for what would happen if you tried to release a big movie in the cinema during the pandemic. So they all postponed and waited for someone else to go first.

It was speculated that it was Universal and not EON who made the decision to scrap the planned November 2020 release. It seemed absurd that anyone had expected the situation to be significantly different in November than it was in April (warnings about a second wave of the virus in the autumn and winter months were not exactly top secret) and equally absurd that another costly marketing campaign was launched. Cinema chains called it a fiasco. They were counting on Bond 25 to save their jobs. The new release date was announced as April 2021. There was though no firm guarantee that this release date would prove any more feasible than the ones that had gone before.

'Our movie industry was just about keeping its morale steady,' wrote Peter Bradshaw in the Guardian. 'It was enforcing perfectly workable rules on sanitising and physical distancing and not subject to those closures taking theatre and live entertainment to the cliff edge. The pilot light of big-screen cinema culture was flickering. But it was still alight. But this is a serious blow. If it is really true that Cineworld will close 128 cinemas, putting 5,500 jobs at risk (and it is not simply a scare-story negotiating ploy leaked to the press alongside the company's official letter to the culture secretary Oliver Dowden demanding action) then this is potentially devastating. For the first time, everyone in the industry is beginning to entertain the queasy thought: what if our cinema industry is like vaudeville? Or silent movies? Or evensong – that once widespread middle-Britain churchgoing habit wiped out by TV? Is cinemagoing finished? A loss-leader adjunct to the home entertainment industry that's long been vulnerable to infection?

'I think the answer is still no. But the other question is: who is to blame for the Cineworld debacle? Big blockbuster movies are routinely nicknamed "tentpoles" for a reason. They keep the whole big top upright. The announcement is that the new James Bond film, No Time to Die, will come out next spring (a transparently vague and unreliable promise) having been already delayed from the spring of this year. It is enraging that Eon (the Bond producers) have lost their nerve so spectacularly, pulling the movie on which the industry had been relying – the big-screen exhibitors that have been supporting and nurturing the 007 franchise since the 60s. It was just as dismaying for the industry that Disney released their high-profile live-action entertainment Mulan to streaming services. But somehow Disney wasn't stringing us along in quite the same way.

'Of course, the whole Bond franchise is a business: we're not talking about a state-subsidised schools workshop tour of Romeo and Juliet. Bond movies are profitable entertainments or they are nothing, and they are produced in an unsentimental way by people who, let's not forget, aren't to blame for coronavirus. And yes, of course, Covid-19 might be with us for so long that this proposed delay might not be as significant as it now appears. But that will be no consolation to Cineworld employees losing their jobs right now. And like it or not, those James Bond extravaganzas – enjoyable, exciting, reactionary, daft – are consumed in a slightly sentimental spirit, and the company has effectively been trading, at least partly, on our pride in a globally popular Brit product. Cinema, like all forms of show business, needs chutzpah and courage, and this year the only big-league players to have really shown this are Christopher Nolan and Warner Brothers who boldly released their mega-action thriller Tenet into cinemas. Eon has reportedly been unnerved by the lacklustre box-office numbers for Tenet, and this long delay is apparently their idea of playing it safe.

'But it isn't simply that this line of thinking discounts the possibility that No Time to Die could have built on the initial steps taken by Tenet; it is the assumption that everything will pretty much be the same next year. Will it? Or will the Bond delay and the Cineworld closure trigger a wave of anxiety that will undermine so many other areas of the service industry and the economy generally? It could be the wing flap not of a butterfly but a pterodactyl. It is possible that Cineworld might reconsider – and the James Bond franchise itself could reconsider, too. In the meantime, we have to remember that most cinemas are still open and they are showing really good films. "Use it or lose it" is an annoying cliche. But we're staring loss in the face.'

Daniel Craig appeared on The Tonight Show and said the delay was for the best. You could forgive him if he'd almost entirely forgotten making No Time To Die by now. That night at Pinewood when they drank cocktails in his trailer to mark the end of shooting must have been starting to feel like an awfully long time ago. Craig said they wanted to release the film when everyone would be able to see it safely at the same time. Fans would just have to be patient. Regarding the Tom Hardy rumours, Barbara Broccoli was quoted in Total Film at this time as saying - "I always say: you can only be in love with one person at a time. Once the film's come out, then some time will pass, and then we'll have to get on to the business of the future. But for now, we just cannot think about anything beyond Daniel."

No Time To Die was obviously a unique Bond film because it required two promotional campaigns (and will clearly require more promotion in the future). The second promotional campaign was aided by the constant drip feed of interviews and No Time To Die special features that had been prepared months in advance. The campaign for No Time To Die was a reminder of the truly international appeal of the James Bond franchise. There were magazine specials and interviews from North America to Europe to China to Japan and beyond. The number of posters for the film was remarkable. This was generally though one area in the marketing where EON needed to pull their socks up. Some of the posters for the Connery and Moore eras were spectacular and iconic (take a look at the posters for films like Thunderball and The Spy Who Loved Me). The poster art for the Brosnan and Craig eras though often left something to be desired.

The IMAX poster of Craig on a motorbike was shoddy and generic indeed. A black and white poster featuring Bond and Swann in a car was more arresting but gave one little clue that this was a Bond film. Better was a more traditional collage featuring Bond and characters from the film. Daniel Craig seemed happy in the press interviews once the film was completed. He seemed to be pleased with the film and relieved that he would no longer have to take a battering on the set of a Bond film again. The trailers and first clip from the film (of Bond in a bridge foot chase in Italy) showed that Craig had put through the mill again when it came to stunts. It was hard at times to pick up a completely consistent tone from the trailers and teasers. There was clearly more of the angsty drama of the Craig era but the glider sequence looked like something out of Die Another Day. The glimpses of the submarine base were a throwback to the spectacular sets of Ken Adam on the classic Bond films while the Italy sequences made No Time To Die look a lot like another Sam Mendes film.

The hope was that Cary Fukunaga had brought all of these elements together into a coherent and satisfying whole. More interviews continued to abound - even as the delays to the release date continued. Playlist reported that Safin's scars were a result of radiation and that Malek had refused to give a straight answer when he was asked if his character was really Dr No. Cary Fukunaga promised that Safin would be a formidable villain. "Once we got into Christoph Waltz/Blofeld territory, you can't go small again. We had to think bigger. It's tricky because you don't want to make a cliché supervillain, but you have to make someone that's threatening not only to Bond and the people he loves but to the world at large." Meanwhile, a late 2020 magazine feature seemed to confirm that Nomi was 007 in the film.

There was naturally a lot of speculation about the possibility of No Time To Die going to streaming platforms and giving up on a cinema release. It was hard to see how the film could make a significant amount of money even if it was released in 2021. It was going to be a long time before cinemas went back to business as usual. The big streaming platforms would obviously have bitten their own arm off to get the exclusive rights to No Time To Die. At the end of October 2020 it was reported that the major streaming giants had offered $600 million for the streaming rights to No Time To Die. When one considers that the last Bond film Spectre made about $800 to $900 million from its theatrical run then this offer was not to be sneezed at.

In fact, a lot of people though that, from a business point of view, it actually made a lot of sense. MGM could get a big chunk of their money back in one fail swoop and pick up more from streaming than No Time To Die figured to make from a restricted cinema release. MGM would even have had the option, once the streaming contract expired (one year was the alleged period for the rights) to give No Time To Die a special cinema release in 2022 to celebrate the anniversary of the

Bond series.

'Apple, Netflix and other streaming services explored the possibility of acquiring No Time to Die, the upcoming James Bond movie that was originally slated to debut last April,' reported Variety. 'The film's release has been postponed multiple times, with the Daniel Craig vehicle moving back to November before being pushed into 2021 as the number of coronavirus cases kept growing. MGM, the studio behind the film, reportedly lost between $30 million to $50 million due to the delays, insiders said. Bloomberg first reported the discussions, which have been the topic du jour in Hollywood this week. Other studios, such as Paramount and Sony, have raked in tens of millions by selling movies like "Greyhound," "Coming 2 America" and "Without Remorse" to streaming services while the exhibition sector continues to struggle during the pandemic. "We do not comment on rumours. The film is not for sale. The film's release has been postponed until April 2021 in order to preserve the theatrical experience for moviegoers," an MGM spokesperson told Variety.

'However, multiple insiders at rival studios and companies said that a possible Bond sale was explored overtly, and believe that MGM was at least open to the possibility of unloading their crown jewel for a princely sum. The studio was said to be looking for a deal of roughly $600 million — a price tag that was deemed too rich for two of the free-spending streaming services. A sale of this magnitude would be led exclusively by Kevin Ulrich, the chairman and CEO of MGM's majority owner Anchorage Capital Group, insiders said. It's unclear if producers Barbara Broccoli and Michael G. Wilson, who exert control of the series through their company Eon, would sign off on the deal. Universal Pictures, which has foreign distribution rights to No Time to Die, would have to be made whole in any possible sale and reimbursed for any expenses the studio incurred.

'That the parties involved would explore a streaming sale is notable, given that the film was the first tentpole to move release dates before coronavirus was upgraded to a global pandemic — making it an early indicator that even the iconic spy and ladies man would not save us from the viral event. Moving No Time to Die to a streaming service poses some logistical challenges. The film costs more than $250 million to produce and has lined up several promotional partnerships to help defray those costs — including Land Rover, Omega watches and Heineken. Those companies may have been expecting the film to hit theaters and might not be thrilled with a streaming-only bow. Coming 2 America's sale to Amazon, for instance, was contingent on making sure that its promotional partners, McDonald's and Crown Royal, were on board with the change in plans.'

There were a sizeable number of Bond fans by now who were tired of waiting for No Time To Die and would have been happy to sacrifice the traditional cinema release simply to get access to the film in the comfort of their own homes. One obvious problem though with the option of releasing No Time To Die straight to streaming platforms was piracy. As soon as the film was released to a big streaming platform than HD copies would then appear on those Putlocker style illegal streaming sites. Even if you did take the streaming option there were still pitfalls and disadvantages. It wasn't simply a case of taking a suitcase full of money from some streaming giant and thinking that all the financial considerations had been solved in one fail swoop.

There were Bond fans too in the other camp. Those who felt saddened by the thought of a Bond film going straight to streaming and preferred to wait until they had a chance to see the film on the big screen - as it was intended. Barbara Broccoli has always been in the latter camp rather than the former. Broccoli had never liked the idea of No Time To Die cutting its losses and going to streaming services. She wanted the tradition and prestige of a cinema release. You could argue that it would cheapen the Bond brand for one of the films to go straight to streaming (even if it was for unusual and understandable reasons).

Broccoli was right in that Bond is (ordinarily) too big for streaming but these were not ordinary times. One sensed there was tension between MGM and Barbara Broccoli over what to do with No Time To Die. MGM wanted to mitigate the financial damage and were prepared to explore alternative options but Broccoli was more interested in the prestige of the Bond series. It was reported that MGM hadn't even told Broccoli they were exploring streaming options. In the midst of all this corporate intrigue, Barbara Broccoli was once again proving to be an admirably strong and determined custodian of the franchise her late father had created.

Variety reported at this time that No Time To Die had a total budget of $301 million and that $66 million had been spent so far in marketing costs. Movieweb reported that the ongoing delays to releasing No Time To Die were costing MGM one million dollars a month in interest. 'MGM is suffering. Every major distributor at this point has a pile of unreleased expensive movies. The pile grows larger by the day. These films are inventory. They are sitting there with no return on their investment. Even with low interest rates, the interest costs are piling up.' Cary Fukunaga was philosophical about the delays himself. As he rightly pointed out, there were more important things in the world to worry about today than when No Time To Die was going to be released.

The decision to postpone No Time To Die again was more than vindicated when Europe experienced an increase in cases of coronavirus. Many countries in Europe went back into a lockdown. There was obviously a desire to release No Time To Die in 2020 but it was absolutely impossible. Many big films in 2020 like Wonder Woman 1984, Black Widow, and Ghostbusters: Afterlife had long since pushed themselves back to 2021 - which was no sure thing either. The horror sequel Halloween Kills had been pushed back an entire year to Halloween 2021. In the grand scheme of things, the release of a James Bond film was insignificant and unimportant when set against the health of people. Fans would simply have to be patient.

CHAPTER EIGHT - JAMES BOND WILL RETURN

The one thing we had learned by now about the James Bond brand is that it was completely indestructible. No Time To Die will eventually and inevitably be followed by more Bond films. You could be sure of that. If you built a time machine and went forward fifty years into the future, someone, somewhere, would be making a Sherlock Holmes film. Someone would probably be making a Batman film. You can bet your life that someone would be making a James Bond film too. Bond is one of those mythic characters who never goes away. He is simply rebooted and passed on from generation to generation and era to era. There will be many actors in the future who will have their moment in the spotlight as the latest Bond. Maybe one day Bond might move to television or streaming in a prestige miniseries format or reboot itself back into the Cold War. Perhaps they might start remaking the old films but this time use the Ian Fleming plots more faithfully. All of these things will doubtless be considered in the decades to come.

For now, James Bond is still a phenomenon of cinema and it is on the big screen where, once things eventually get back to something approaching normality, he will return. The fictional James Bond has survived steel teethed giants, strongmen with razor brimmed hats, Spectre assassins, and a million death defying situations. The film franchise is no less an expert when it comes to escapology. The Bond series has survived litigation, a rival 'renegade' Bond film, endless copycats, the departure of its original lead actor, the departure of the original co-producer, and several recastings of Bond himself. The franchise will ultimately defeat the coronavirus and outlast us all.

The remarkable thing about the Bond series is that 25 films

have spawned from what one would presume to be a fairly constrictive world and genre - the spy action adventure thriller. It is true that, unavoidably, there has been a lot of repetition in the Bond series. Casino scenes, the Aston Martin, ski chases. A View To a Kill borrows the plot of Goldfinger with Silicon Valley replacing Fort Knox. Moonraker's plot is a rehash of the plot of The Spy Who Loved Me. Bond has a signature gun in Spectre - just like he had a signature gun in Licence To Kill. And so on.

The advantage Bond films had over other franchises though was to always set themselves in the present day - or 'five minutes into the future' as Cubby Broccoli liked to say. You basically get the same film but dressed up in new fashions and technology. It's a formula that has worked surprisingly well. "People always ask if Bond is relevant," said Barbara Broccoli. "I remember when the Berlin Wall came down. Just before we made Goldeneye. Everyone said, 'The world's at peace, why do we need Bond?' Well, the world wasn't at peace, and as long as the world needs a hero, Bond is going to be relevant'.

It's difficult to know what history will make of No Time To Die once it finally becomes the past - as opposed to that film that took FOREVER to come out. It is possible that the real world problems which blighted numerous attempts to release the film will be as prevalent in retrospectives of No Time To Die as anything that actually happened in the actual film. This would be an atypical film in the franchise because it capped an era in a way that had never really been attempted in the series before. A View To a Kill, for example, has no sense of being the last Roger Moore film. At the time they didn't know if it was definitely Roger's last film but at 57 years of age they must have suspected that it probably would be. Even so, there is no pause for reflection or any nostalgia in A View To a Kill. It's simply another Bond film with Roger Moore.

Die Another Day gives no hint that this is Pierce Brosnan's last film because at the time it was obviously assumed that Brosnan would be back. Licence To Kill has not the barest hint of being Timothy Dalton's last film because at the time they had no idea the series was about to go into mothballs and were already making vague plans for the third Dalton adventure. Even when Sean Connery made his one-shot return to play Bond in Diamonds Are Forever it was a purely stand alone adventure with no reference to the past. There wasn't any attempt to market or reference the fact that this was Connery's last go around. The reason for this was presumably that United Artists still hadn't given up on the idea of him coming back again. That wasn't going to happen. Connery only did Diamonds Are Forever in the first place so that he could use his one million dollar fee to set up a new charity for young people. He had no intention of playing James Bond again - not for EON anyway.

The one interesting thing they used to do in Bond films that connected the actors was to reference the death of Bond's wife in On Her Majesty's Secret Service. Roger Moore's Bond is noticeably touchy in The Spy Who Loved Me when Barbara Bach as Anya Amasova mentions that he was once married. The PTS of For Your Eyes Only begins with Roger's Bond placing flowers on the grave of his wife. This scene was actually written for a new Bond actor because they didn't think Roger was coming back. It was left in though and provides a nice little 'human' moment for Roger's Bond. In 1989's Licence To Kill, Timothy Dalton smiles weakly and refuses to accept a garter from Della when she tells him that he'll be the next to get married. These little moments in the Moore and Dalton films were a nice touch and connected the cinematic Bonds in a very understated but effective way. By the time of the Brosnan and Craig films, the references to Bond's wife were dropped. Too much time had passed. Craig's Bond had a completely different background and past.

No Time To Die then was fairly unique in the way that it was marketed as Daniel Craig's last film. It was hard to think of this ever happening in the Bond franchise before. No Time To Die was even written with instructions to actually acknowledge this fact and bring all of Craig's films together into some sort of ending. In terms of years, Craig is the longest serving Bond. It feels like he has been around for an awfully long time. However, as we have seen, the films had such long gaps in his era at times that Roger Moore's record of seven films was never really under serious threat.

The reaction to Craig's casting in 2005 was underwhelming. Most people had never heard of him. Craig gave a poor impression at his first press conference by chewing gum and not displaying much in the way of personality. The Sun called him James Bland. Barbara Broccoli and Michael G Wilson were dismayed by the negative press. A website (which still exists) was set up to protest at his casting. The website complained that Craig was 'short, craggy, and blond' and looked more like Putin than James Bond. A decade and a half on, Daniel Craig could look back with satisfaction. He had lasted much longer than anyone expected.

Daniel Craig had steered the Bond franchise through another era and was ready to pass the baton on. Bond was still big business. It was still in good health and still apparently indestructible. Craig's advice for his replacement was simple. "Don't **** it up. Leave it better than you found it." He said he didn't care who his replacement was. That was something for Barbara Broccoli to worry about. Craig felt he could make a decent fist of playing any part. He was looking forward to new challenges in his post-Bond career. There was even talk of a Knives Out sequel. History suggested that Craig was right to be optimistic. With the exception of George Lazenby (who wasn't really an actor) and Roger Moore (who was more interested in his duties as a UNICEF Goodwill Ambassador than acting in the 1990s and beyond), all of the Bond actors enjoyed eclectic and fruitful careers after their time as 007 came to an end.

Sean Connery was still busy and still a huge star right up until his retirement in 2003. Pierce Brosnan was busier than ever after Die Another Die. In 2010 he gave one of his best performances in the Roman Polanski film The Ghost Writer. Timothy Dalton never stopped working after Bond and, thanks to the enduring cult appeal of the 1981 film Flash Gordon and new roles in projects as diverse as Hot Fuzz, Doctor who, and Penny Dreadful, he even threatened to become something of a national treasure. It was (unsurprisingly) George Lazenby who struggled the most post-Bond out of the 007 actors. He appeared in a couple of Hong Kong kung-fu films, some B-movie thrillers and chillers, and Australian television movies. A movie called Universal Soldier, about a hippie mercenary in London, was partly funded by Lazenby but was an obscure flop. Lazenby had failed to deduce the simple fact that no actor was bigger than Bond. Lazenby assumed he was a star after OHMSS but James Bond was the star. By leaving the Bond series after one film, Lazenby torpedoed his own career before it had even begun.

When he left the Bond series, George Lazenby assumed he would be awash with offers. The problem for Lazenby though is that he wasn't an actor. His performance in OHMSS, guided by the director Peter Hunt and the supporting class of Diana Rigg, was remarkably good given his inexperience. But he had no acting career to fall back on. Aside from a Big fry chocolate commercial, Lazenby had no acting CV at all before Bond. Connery, Moore, Dalton, Brosnan, and Craig were all professional actors when they were hired as Bond. They all had, to varying degrees, a body of work (Connery was actually the most inexperienced out of the five because he was only 31 when he became Bond) behind them and a career to fall back on. Lazenby was never willing to serve his apprenticeship - something that the other Bond actors all had to do before they were rich and famous.

The remarkable thing about Lazenby's departure from Bond is that he genuinely seemed to believe he was leaving a sinking ship. His agent told him that James Bond was conservative and dated. A relic of the fifties and sixties that would wheeze on for a couple more films and then be consigned to history. It was one of the stupidest pieces of advice anyone could ever be unfortunate enough to receive. Many decades later, Lazenby could probably allow himself to see the funny side as he signed autographs at Bond conventions and did yet another interview about his time as James Bond. Fads and eras (not to mention actors) come and go but James Bond was indestructible and forever. Lazenby now knew that only too well.

Daniel Craig had little to worry about as he finally looked to a future beyond James Bond. He was financially secure and could now pick and choose projects as he pleased. He would not be short of offers as the next chapter in the James Bond franchise moved ahead without him. The Daniel Craig era of Bond could be described as a game of two halves. Casino Royale and Skyfall were warmly received while Quantum of Solace and Spectre met a lukewarm and even negative reception. No Time To Die then, in a sense, would have the deciding vote. The reaction to the film could tilt the perception of the Craig era as a whole in either direction.

We come full circle now by wondering if the experiment of the Craig 'miniseries' with its connected and more serious ('gritty' is the awful word that often gets thrown around) approach was actually a success or not. Did it hamstring the Craig films or make them more interesting? That is a purely subjective matter and not easy to answer. 'There are two groups of people given to lengthy discussion about characters named Mr White,' wrote techradar. 'Reservoir Dogs fans, and the Double-o division of MI6. All in all, when No Time To Die releases, Bond will have spent 14 years and five films tracing the steps and life story of the elusive Spectre lieutenant. Yet all but the most dedicated Bond nuts would struggle to remember anything about him beyond his favourite colour. I wouldn't imagine that his actor, Jesper Christensen, gets recognized a lot in the street. You might say he's emblematic of Spectre's capacity to be everywhere yet unseen; that sounds like a line you might hear in one of the Craig-era Bond films.

'But really, it's an indictment of just how flimsy and forgettable the larger arc of those movies has been. The idea was always exciting in principle – that each of Craig's missions wouldn't exist in isolation, but contribute to a slow build of intrigue, every villain part of a greater conspiracy conducted by the criminal organization that featured throughout Ian Fleming's novels and the early Bond films of the '60s. In reality this background plot has been inconsistently applied, like a slapdash paint job – sometimes clumping over otherwise smooth stretches of film, sometimes fading into nothing. It cannot truly hope to tie these movies together since, fundamentally, they don't belong together. They might all star the same actor, but the Craig years have run the gamut tonally.

'Any lingering sense that Bond was 'rebooted' when Craig stepped aboard can be quickly picked apart; two thirds of Casino Royale's writing team, Neal Purvis and Robert Wade, are the men who brought Die Another Day into the world. Director Martin Campbell was brought in as a safe pair of hands, having ushered Pierce Brosnan into the series a decade earlier. While Casino Royale succeeded in stripping away the bloat of the Brosnan era, it did so by returning to the same well. These are not films of a kind, then, and moreover, serialization has not been kind to them. Spectre in particular suffers for its dedication to the cause, trawling through the history of the White family as if the viewer had accidentally agreed to sit through their holiday photos. When Blofeld claims to have been the author of all Bond's pain, you suspect he's self-published. Is it really so shocking that an MI6 agent has had numerous encounters with an organization that professes to control all crime? You might as well claim responsibility for making binmen's hands dirty.

'There's no doubt that continuity has imbued some series with a powerful, slow-burn excitement. Avengers: Endgame became the highest-grossing movie of all time partly on its individual merits, and partly because it promised the conclusion to a story told across 22 films. But Marvel works at a different cadence to Bond; an overarching plot doesn't necessarily benefit movies that can be four or five years apart. You're probably not even living in the same property you inhabited during the release of Spectre. Being asked to remember what happened in Quantum of Solace feels more like a cruel reminder of mortality than the thrilling unfurling of an ongoing story. Speaking of which, poor Craig was catapulted from the first kills of Bond's career to dinosaur status in the space of just three films. He's spent a full half of his tenure as an "old dog", used as a vehicle to explore themes of legacy and redundancy. If his prime years ever happened, we didn't see them.'

If one looks at the Craig films individually, you can construct a case for the connected elements becoming more of a hindrance than a strength. Casino Royale had the advantage of being a fresh slate. It had no baggage and a sense of purpose. Casino Royale had an Ian Fleming novel to crib from and a 'concept' in that it depicted a wet behind the ears Bond. Quantum of Solace sought to be a direct continuation of Casino Royale but it had no idea how to do this or where to take the story next. It ended up spinning its wheels (quite literally) in a number of incoherent badly edited action sequences. Skyfall detached itself somewhat from the continuation structure and came up with a new concept. Bond is now burnt out and feeling his age. This is ludicrous on the face of it (he was a rookie two films ago!) but it gives Skyfall a sense of purpose and a theme around which to tell its story.

Spectre tried to connect itself to Skyfall but Sam Mendes was now out of ideas. He loses the 'burnt out' Bond angle and tries to make Craig more like the traditional Bond of yore. It doesn't work. Mendes and Craig are not a good fit for a zippy fun traditional Bond film. The third act of Spectre, which seeks to connect all of the Craig films, is weak and unconvincing. It feels like an afterthought. Mendes had no concept or theme for Spectre and it shows. This is why Bond films were traditionally episodic by nature.

It always seems a little unfair when it is reported that Daniel Craig was the first actor to try and do something less flippant with the part of James Bond. Craig is often written about as if he was the first person to try and make Bond more human. Lauding Craig as the first person to try and flesh Bond out somewhat or humanise him seems inaccurate in light of Timothy Dalton's darker and more Fleming faithful Bond (in The Living Daylights at least). 'For me the name is Dalton, Timothy Dalton, wrote Gwladys Fouché in the Guardian Film Blog in 2006. 'He was dark, he was ruthless, and he managed to show precisely what Bond was all about: a merciless, calculating, professional assassin. Is it inappropriate to mention that he was also unbelievably good-looking and charismatic? So why is he still treated as though he massacred the role? Timothy Dalton was a great 007. Ironically, the very characteristics that got Dalton slammed are the very same things that the Bond producers are praising Daniel Craig for. On and on, they have said they want Bond to be closer to the original Ian Fleming character. They want him to be grittier, darker and less jokey. What they really want, it seems, is to have Dalton back.'

George Lazenby's 007 ended a film crying his eyes out at the death of his wife. How much more human can you get? It's not as if no one ever tried to do anything dark, dramatic, or emotional before Barbara Broccoli and Daniel Craig took over the franchise. Has the Daniel Craig era gone too far in an angsty direction? One could argue that James Bond actually becomes less interesting the more you know about him. The cinematic James Bond is traditionally a male fantasy proxy - a big screen Milk Tray Man. Bond is mysterious and compelling but fun. You can't really imagine emotional angst or continuity in the Connery films. These elements would feel strangely out of place.

Angst felt out of place in the Brosnan era too whenever they tried to slip some in. A few times they tried to give Brosnan a small reflective moment where we are supposed to see how difficult it must be to have his job but it just doesn't suit Brosnan's Bond. Brosnan's Bond feels like someone who loves having a licence to kill and roaming around the world! You feel like Brosnan should be in Connery or Moore style fantastical epics like You Only Live Twice or The Spy Who Loved Me - not trying to make Bond human.

The general rule with Bond is that is that, like any long running franchise, it has to adapt and change over time. The series needed a course adjustment after Die Another Day but any phase of Bond has a shelf life. The emotional angst and continuity of the Craig films had a shelf life too and No Time To Die was a risky film in a sense as it was going to see how elastic the experiment of an ongoing story in the Bond films really was. Did we really need a fifth film with Craig's Bond? Was there anywhere left to go with this phase of 007? If the film was really good then any potential fan weariness over the constant 'this time it's personal and here's some more of that story thread from four years ago you've probably forgotten anyway' angle to the Craig films wouldn't be a factor. No Time To Die had a tricky task but not an impossible one. As we said in chapter one, No Time To Die simply had to justify its own existence. As long as it did that it would be fine.

A strange phenomenon with James Bond actors is that their Bond performances seem to be more harshly judged once they no longer have the role and are consigned to history. Sean Connery, as the original and most would contend the best, is of course immune to this retrospective reappraisal. Timothy Dalton was lauded in 1987 for taking the films back to the books. Nowadays, most people tend to assume that Dalton must have been terrible because he only made a couple of films. Roger Moore made more films than any other Bond actor but you'd think he was hopeless and laughable in the part if read some retrospective articles about Roger. It is very fashionable to slate the Roger Moore era and yet the Moore era actually brought countless new fans to the franchise because his films were fun and amusing.

The biggest victim of retrospective reappraisal is surely Pierce Brosnan. Brosnan was deemed pretty much the perfect person to be Bond in 1994. Martin Campbell said that Brosnan playing Bond in GoldenEye was such a no brainer that they didn't even bother to test any other actors. No one seemed to have any vocal complaints about Brosnan from 1995 to 2002.

And yet, when Brosnan was replaced and became an ex-Bond, he was retrospectively judged to have been terrible in the part. It will then be interesting indeed to see what the retrospective consensus on Daniel Craig might be in ten years when he is merely an ex-Bond and someone else is established in the part. The debate though over eras and films was the beauty of the Bond series. Some fans love Timothy Dalton's darker and more brooding take on the character. Some fans love the tongue-in-cheek humour and fun of the Roger Moore films. Some fans love the 'rough diamond' Bond of the Daniel Craig era. And some fans love all the eras - warts and all.

There are certain things (plenty of action, amazing stunts, beautiful locations, beautiful women, fast cars, villains, swanky casinos, high fashion) people will always expect from a James Bond film but there is no one specific way to approach and make a Bond film. It can be reinvented or rebooted. It can be completely changed by recasting the lead. It can be connected or episodic. It can be light or dark. It can be serious or tongue-in-cheek. It can be fantastical or grounded. No Time To Die is simply another part of the tapestry. When the dust firmly settles on No Time To Die the attention will turn to Bond 26. The character will go and on - constantly reinvented and recast for new generations. Whatever happens in the series the fans are always assured of one thing. James Bond WILL return.

CPSIA information can be obtained
at www.ICGtesting.com
Printed in the USA
LVHW020706221021
701184LV00020B/1410

9 781393 764014